View from the
Bronze Age

View from the Bronze Age

Mycenaean and Phoenician Discoveries at Kition

by Vassos Karageorghis

E. P. Dutton & Co., Inc.
New York · 1976

First published in the U.S.A. in 1976 by
E. P. Dutton & Co., Inc.

Copyright © 1976 by
Thames and Hudson, Ltd., London

All rights reserved
Printed in Great Britain

First Edition

10 9 8 7 6 5 4 3 2 1

ISBN: 0-525-22866-7

Library of Congress Catalog Card Number:
75-42513

Contents

The investigation of the cardinal Bronze Age of Cyprus has now been pursued with varying degrees of system and acuteness for more than a century by a sequence of explorers ranging from British, French, Swedish and German to Cypriots themselves, whose publications already constitute an aggregation of high distinction. More recently the present series of New Aspects of Antiquity published by Messrs Thames and Hudson has been enriched by reports of the now familiar excavations of the semi-Homeric tombs of Salamis uncovered by the late Dr P. Dikaios and his active successor as Director of Antiquities, Dr Vassos Karageorghis; and now, to the famous city-site of Enkomi, discovered on the eastern side of the island in 1934 and subsequently excavated by Professor Claude Schaeffer and his colleagues, must be added the revolutionary Late Bronze Age harbour town of Kition on the south coast beneath the modern town of Larnaca. The site lies close to a natural inner harbour approached through a navigable channel and within reach of deposits of salt and of copper ore. Nor is this all. Adjacent quarters of the burgeoning city have revealed both sacred and industrial structures of the Late Bronze Age, throwing light upon associated metallurgical and religious aspects of Phoenician colonization from the ninth century BC onwards as a counterpart to marked cultural changes wrought by Achaean colonization, without obscuring pronounced Near Eastern usages, whether in temple-planning or in the cultivation of sacred gardens such as have been identified elsewhere at the temple of Aphrodite at Paphos and in the XIX Dynasty in Egypt. Indeed the indications of sacred gardens at Kition itself seem to be the oldest of their kind found so far in the Mediterranean region. Less certainly associated with the cults of certain Kition shrines is a large number of stone anchors reused in building-construction, no doubt vestiges of the sea-trade of the port but possessed also of some religious significance.

Above all, religious remains have included a great inscribed temple of Astarte, whose architectural vestiges are claimed to be those of the largest Phoenician shrine ever found. The goddess was the supreme divinity of the Phoenician world hereabouts for something like 500 years, until indeed the fall of the Phoenician Dynasty of the city at the end of the fourth century BC, when the last king was killed by Ptolemy I amidst a general conflagration, although the city had already been once destroyed by undefined means before the end of the eleventh century BC. The ancient ceremonies of Astarte are represented by numerous skulls of oxen prepared for priestly service as masks, found on the floor of the temple and recalling the old Cypriote Bronze Age cult of the bull as symbolizing an ancient tradition of fertility. Sacred pits or *bothroi* roundabouts contain offerings to characterize the wealth of the temple at successive phases in the shape of Greek oil-jars, Egyptian scarabs and amulets of various origin and cosmopolitan types, illustrating the temple's widespread appeal in the Near Eastern world. Above all, the continuing and close association of the religion of the great temple and its environs with metallurgy is emphasized by the presence of a workshop for the smelting of copper during the Archaic and Classical periods beside its old east entrance, for the manufacture of holy relics on sale to the numerous pilgrims to the shrine. The necessary ores were obtainable from two neighbouring mines known as Kalavassos and Troulli, the resources of which were shared with Kition between the fifteenth and twelfth centuries BC, and for a lesser period with another Late Bronze Age town of the vicinity known as Hala Sultan Tekké. Industrially and commercially the whole region was of outstanding prosperity, the shadow of which has continued to modern times in spite of the relative poverty of the hinterland hereabouts.

The archaeological interest of Kition thus lies primarily in its prestige as a flourishing branch of Phoenician and secondarily Aegean colonization and industry, with busy harbour-outlets for trade based upon rich local ores and the subsidiary collection and export of salt but with only a modest range of local artistry, though with an abundant religious life (see Chapter VII) and an appreciable range of tomb-furniture, particularly from fourteenth-century chamber-tombs in the courtyards of a number of houses recalling those of Enkomi and the Syrian mainland. The contents of the tombs included a mass of Mycenaean pottery, alabaster vessels, ostrich-eggs, faience and gold jewellery. It is clear that in certain directions the description 'fabulous' which has been applied to Kition in the thirteenth century is no exaggeration. The Cypro–Minoan script, though found there, has not yet been historically useful. Whilst known as one of the island kingdoms from the Classical period onwards, it has no foundation legend but is on the other hand alleged to have been established by Belos, king of Sidon, thus emphasizing its focus in the Near East.

MORTIMER WHEELER

Foreword and Acknowledgments

During the last twenty-five years or so research on the Late Bronze Age of the Eastern Aegean has experienced an unprecedented impetus. The decipherment of the Mycenaean Linear B script has opened new horizons in Aegean studies and intensive field work in the Near East has emphasized the crucial importance of Near Eastern culture in the development of Mediterranean civilization from the Late Bronze Age onwards. It is now obvious that the area from South Italy to the Syro–Palestinian coast is one archaeological entity in which the artificial barriers created by nineteenth-century scholarship can no longer be defended.

It is this new climate in archaeological research that has fostered excavations of Late Bronze Age sites in Cyprus during recent years. The discovery of the ancient city of Enkomi on the east coast of the island in 1934 and its subsequent excavation had already revealed the importance of the site as a major centre of art and architecture which developed under the influence of the Aegean and the Near East; it also emphasized the role of Cyprus as the stepping-stone between the great cultures of East and West, and as a 'melting pot' wherein these two cultures mingled to create something new.

Whereas the discovery of the town of Enkomi was due to both chance and the intuition of its excavator, Professor C. F. A. Schaeffer,[1] the discovery of Late Bronze Age Kition in 1959 was due solely to chance, though its existence was indicated as early as 1930.[2] Fourteen years of excavations at Kition have revolutionized our knowledge about its ancient past.[3] For the first time its importance as a major harbour town of the Late Bronze Age has come to light, whereas it was earlier considered a Phoenician foundation of the ninth–eighth centuries BC.[4] At the same time excavation has revealed a sacred and industrial quarter of the Late Bronze Age town which throws new light on metallurgy in Cyprus and its association with religion. In a relatively small area impressive architectural remains of temples have been found adjacent to spacious workshops and next to Cyclopean fortifications. At the same time, however, the Phoenician aspect of Kition, from the ninth century B C onwards, may now be studied anew from tangible evidence connected with the Phoenician colonists. The great temple of Astarte, whose imposing architectural remains make it the largest Phoenician temple ever found, identified with the goddess by a long Phoenician inscription, is but one important element in the study of the presence of the Phoenicians in their first Western Colony.

The new archaeological evidence about Kition illustrates the importance and fame which this city, and through it the whole of Cyprus, had for Near Eastern peoples. The whole island is known in the Bible (in passages which may date to the eighth and seventh centuries B C) as Kittim, evidently after Kition.[5] In Genesis, Elishah, one of the 'sons of Javan', is referred to as brother of Kittim. The latter is obviously to be connected with Kition, and there are scholars who suggest that Elishah should be connected with Alashiya, the prehistoric name of Cyprus. In a passage in Ezekiel, 'benches of ivory inlaid in boxwood' are said to come from the 'isles of Kittim', whereas the 'isles of Elishah' are mentioned as the source of 'blue and purple cloth'. There are several other biblical references to Kittim which are worth mentioning. One refers to the naval power of Kittim; in the prophecy of Balaan, Balak is warned that 'ships shall come from the coast of Kittim, and they shall afflict Ashur, and shall afflict Eber, and he also shall come to destruction'. Perhaps the best known biblical reference is that in Isaiah, dated to the second half of the eighth century B C, where he prophesies of what shall befall Tyre, the metropolis of Kition: 'Howl, ye ships of Tarshish; for it is laid waste, so that there is no house, no entering in: from the land of Kittim it is revealed to them.' In a similar passage Isaiah says: 'Thou shall no more rejoice, O oppressed virgin daughter of Sidon; arise, pass over to Kittim; even there shalt thou have no rest.'

If Kition gave its name to the whole of Cyprus, which is referred to as the 'isles of Kittim', it is obvious that Kition was the town *par excellence* which was known to the biblical world, especially as a maritime power. This is not surprising in view of its Phoenician connections, now well attested as a result of excavations.

As work continues no doubt other new discoveries will elucidate both the archaeology and history of the site, though we already have enough material to establish its continuous history from the Late Bronze Age and even earlier, as well as through 600 years of Phoenician domination. The architectural remains of the temples and workshops, their various annexes and courtyards, the city wall and tombs, present enough information for a volume which will illustrate completely new aspects in the history of Kition. We shall not deal here with already known facts about the site, based mainly on the excavations of the Swedish Cyprus Expedition in 1929 and 1930, nor some previous researches, the results of which have mostly been published,[6] but we shall confine ourselves to the period from the earliest phase in the existence of the town down to the end of the fourth century B C, which marks the end of the Phoenician period. A detailed historical account of Kition from the end of the fourth century B C onwards, based mainly on epigraphic, literary and surface survey information, lies outside the scope of the present study.

The publication of this book, at a time when excavation results at Enkomi are published annually, will provide a useful interim comparison between these two major sites of Late Bronze Age Cyprus which often share an identical history and material culture. It will also provide new material for the present renewal of interest in Phoenician studies.

This book was written recently at a time when the island of Cyprus, playing its ancient but perilous role as a bone of contention between East and West, has found itself in the drama of a war and all its tragic consequences. The final touches to the text and the preparation of the illustrations could not have been achieved without the arduous collaboration of a number of colleagues nor without the devotion of the technical staff of the Department of Antiquities, Cyprus. Thanks are due to the Ministry of Communications and Works of the Republic of Cyprus and all the private individuals who contributed generously towards the cost of the excavations at Kition; the civic authorities of Larnaca for their constant support during the excavations; my Master in field archaeology, Sir Mortimer Wheeler, who suggested this book for the New Aspects of Antiquity series of which he is General Editor; the staff of Thames and Hudson for much encouragement and unfailing collaboration; the members of the photographic section of the Department of Antiquities, especially Mr Stelios Nicolaides, who prepared all the photographs; the Surveyors of the Department of Antiquities, Mr Elias Markou and Mr Chrysilios Polykarpou, who prepared the drawings. Mr Markou offered his expert collaboration in the field throughout all the seasons of excavation from 1959 onwards; my foremen and collaborators in the field, Mr Kakoullis Georghiou, Mr Andreas Georghiou and Mr Andreas Savva. The first two named also gave much help in preparing the material for publication; the members of the Laboratory of the Cyprus Museum, especially Mr Andreas Papadopoullos and Mr Chrysostomos Paraskeva, who treated objects from the excavation in the Cyprus Museum Laboratory; Miss Ellen Herscher, Miss Jenny Webb and other graduate students, who participated in the latest (1974) campaign of excavations, with whom I discussed very profitably various problems in the field; my secretary, Mrs Maroulla Tsouri, who very patiently typed the manuscript. Last, but not least, I would like to express my gratitude to Mr John Hadjisavvas, Assistant Record Keeper in the Department of Antiquities, who with competence and devotion helped with the illustrations and in all kinds of technical problems during the preparation of this book.

Department of Antiquities,
Nicosia.

I The Site of Kition

Fig. 1

The south coast of Cyprus with its natural harbours, protected from the strong winds and nearer to Egypt and the Syro–Palestinian coast than any other part of the island, attracted the early Cypriots from the Neolithic period onwards. The sites of Khirokitia, Kalavassos, Sotira, Erimi, with their important Neolithic and Chalcolithic remains, lie all along the coast. Here also are the rich mining areas of Kalavassos and Troulli which must have contributed to the wealth of numerous sites during the Bronze Age. The emergence of settlements along the south and east coasts of the island as trading centres favoured by the *pax Aegyptiaca*, and the Mycenaean expansion to the Eastern Mediterranean, brought about the climax in the development of a chain of major harbour towns, known mainly from the wealth of their tombs. Only Enkomi and now Kition have revealed architectural remains.

Fig. 2

Kition lies in a particularly favoured area, within a large protected bay to the south of a once marshy region inside the bay, which provided a partly natural and partly artificial, well-protected harbour. Within a short distance to the south of Kition is the Salt Lake of Larnaca, on the west bank of which flourished one of the largest, if not the largest, Late Bronze Age towns of Cyprus from the sixteenth to the twelfth centuries BC. This site, known as Hala Sultan Tekké, is currently being excavated by the Swedish Expedition under Professor P. Åström.[7] The lake provided an inner harbour through a navigable channel, comparable with the marshy region on the northern outskirts of Kition. The exploitation of salt must have been one of the main industries of the region as it is today, as, unlike Enkomi, the town could not depend on an agriculturally rich hinterland. At a short distance to the north-east of Kition lie several other important sites near the village of Pyla (Verghi, Dhekelia and Kokkinokremmos) indicated by the results of very limited excavations.[8]

That so little was known of the early history of Kition is due, we believe, to the fact that the ancient site lies directly beneath the modern town of Larnaca. Foundation trenches for modern building purposes have rarely reached 2 m in depth, though often revealing Hellenistic and Classical remains which lie nearer to the surface. Late Bronze Age remains often lie 3–4 m below the present surface. Moreover there are very few open spaces available for excavation. Only the area of the vast Iron Age necropolis, along the western outskirts of Larnaca, is not yet so densely inhabited and has provided profitable fields for clandestine and amateur excavation over a long period in the past. From this area come the majority of tomb-groups in the Cyprus Museum and the Larnaca District Museum, revealed by emergency excavations during the last twenty years or so, when the town of Larnaca started expanding westwards. Another factor which may have prejudiced the exploration of the earlier archaeological phases of Kition was the universal conviction that Kition was

1 Map of Cyprus showing sites mentioned in the text

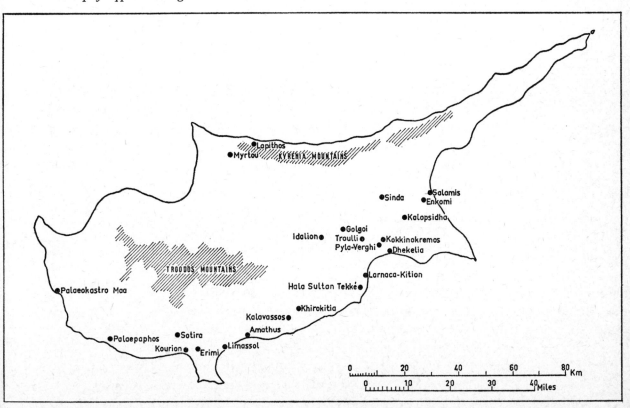

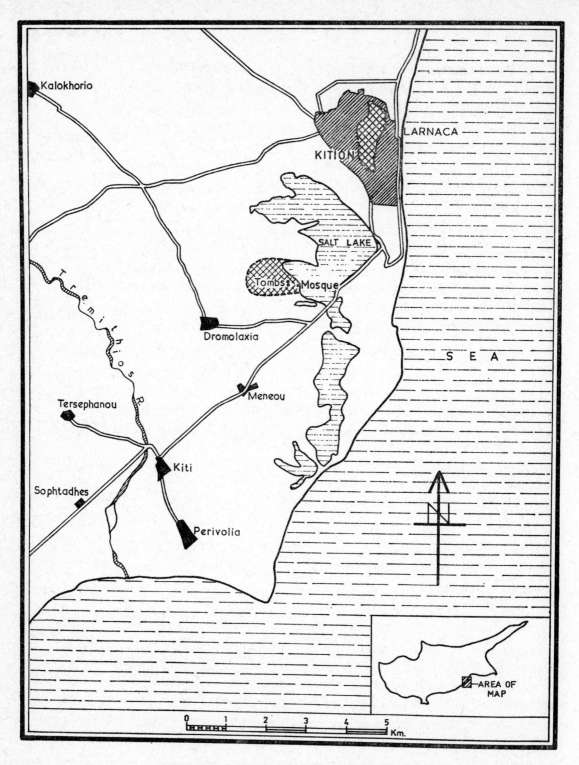

2   Plan of part of the south coast of Cyprus showing the modern town of Larnaca incorporating the site of ancient Kition (cross-hatched); to the south the Salt Lake with the site of the Late Bronze Age town (cross-hatched) on its western bank

Phoenician and did not have an earlier past. This hypothesis was strengthened also by the fact that, of all the kingdoms of the island known from the Classical period, this was almost the only one which did not have a Greek foundation legend, but is said to have been founded by Belos, king of Sidon.[9]

In 1929 and 1930 the Swedish Cyprus Expedition excavated on a limited scale on the Acropolis of Kition at the site of a sanctuary dedicated to Heracles–Melkarth, mainly to 'obtain an archaeologically fixed point for the dating of the Phoenician colonization of Cyprus'.[10] They discovered that the Acropolis of Kition was first inhabited at the end of Late Cypriote III and the beginning of Cypro–Geometric I.[11] Had they extended their excavation they would doubtless have found the earlier remains of the city which date about two centuries earlier to the beginning of the thirteenth century BC.

In 1913 Sir John Myres also excavated on the Acropolis of Kition but he found nothing dating earlier than *c.* 1000 BC except for one 'Late Minoan' sherd.[12] Writing in 1946, he excluded the possibility of the existence of an important Late Bronze Age town at the site of Kition, preferring the theory that Kition succeeded the Late Bronze Age town near the Salt Lake at the beginning of the Iron Age, in the same way as Salamis succeeded Enkomi. Stanley Casson believed that it would be unwise to draw conclusions from the absence of Mycenaean remains at Kition, though he was disturbed by the fact that there was no foundation legend for the town. He prophetically wrote that if Mycenaean objects were found there one day then it would be necessary to revise our theories about Kition.[13]

The most extensive 'excavation', however, and by far the most disastrous to the site, was the operation undertaken in 1879, one year after the British occupation of Cyprus. In order to dry out the marshes around the ancient harbour which were the cause of malaria during the summer months, instructions were given to the Royal Engineers to fill them up by levelling a 'mound of rubbish' close to the marshes. This mound, known as 'Bamboula', was the Acropolis of Kition, no doubt the most prominent and most important site of the ancient town. The magnitude of the catastrophe may be seen in the short report which was submitted by the officer in charge of the operations, and from which a few characteristic extracts are here cited in order to illustrate the kind of buildings which have been lost to archaeology for good:[14]

> As we proceeded at [area] D a wall of very good ashlar masonry began to show itself running inwards and about 10 feet high it however stopped abruptly after about 50' – where the masonry again became rough and coarse – other rough walls in various directions were come across and quantities of good squared stone strewn among the rubbish in astonishing confusion. No plan or design could be recognized in these amorphous masses of masonry. The earth between was generally in layers of different colour and texture with here and there one of ashes and broken earthenware and potsherds in all directions and great quantity at [area] E were found two stones with holes through them fixed in the ground and apparently used for fastening the ships in harbour. . . .

The ashlar blocks of stone, the ashes and the stones with holes through them give an indication of the nature of the buildings which were destroyed. In the area excavated by the Department of Antiquities of Cyprus near the northern part of the city wall, at a short distance west of Bamboula, buildings were found constructed of ashlar blocks which lie directly on foundations made up of stone anchors. These buildings are generally temples dating to the end of the thirteenth century BC and are associated with the first Achaean settlement at Kition (see below). The report continues:

> The earth is everywhere of the same nature full of broken pottery small stone and mortar and evidently the débris of former buildings. The holes running in various directions are in the earth not in masonry and the walls give no clue as to the design or form of the buildings but run aimlessly in all directions and in the most perplexing manner.

Some of the material discovered during these excavations, now in the British Museum, is of Late Bronze Age date, as for instance a 'small model of a bath in dark stone, ornamented with zigzag lines and overlapping sides'. It is in this area that the famous Phoenician inscription on both sides of a marble slab was found which records the accounts of the temple of Astarte at Kition.[15] Reference to this will be made later when we discuss the temple of Astarte excavated recently. Other objects found include a large Ionic capital of local marble, a type common in Cyprus during the Archaic period, and believed to be votive in character. In 1845 the famous stele of Sargon, now in Berlin, was discovered. It refers to the submission to King Sargon II of the kings of Cyprus[16] and must have been erected at Kition in 707 BC. The importance of the lost Acropolis of Kition, a site perhaps far more significant than the monumental sacred and industrial quarter revealed by excavations a short distance to the west of the Acropolis, is thus briefly illustrated.

Excavations of tombs and sanctuaries in the nineteenth century have supplied ample evidence of the Phoenician character of Kition's material culture during the Iron Age.[17] Epigraphic evidence has completed this information, with the temple of Astarte at Kition known from inscriptions.[18] The city wall could be traced at the western part but no date could be given to it without stratigraphical evidence from an excavation. The remains of well-constructed sanctuaries were also indicated. As early as the eighteenth century chroniclers and travellers mention the archaeological remains which were 'daily dug up all round'.[19] They were all impressed by the fine quality of the masonry of these buildings. Drummond admired the 'well squared stones of a prodigious size'; Pococke[20] saw a number of ancient 'sepulchres', the walls of which were 'of excellent workmanship and finished in the most perfect manner'. The site of the harbour, between the Acropolis and the present sea-shore, was also clearly to be seen.[21]

Figs 3, 4

Accidental discoveries made in 1947 and 1957 attested the existence of a much earlier settlement in this region, dated to the Early and Middle Bronze Ages.[22] In 1957 a tomb was found on an area of elevated ground about 1 km north-west of the Acropolis of Kition near the church of Ayios Prodromos. This site, surrounded by marshy land (dried up in 1879), may have been a kind of islet in antiquity, but it requires exploration in order to determine whether it was

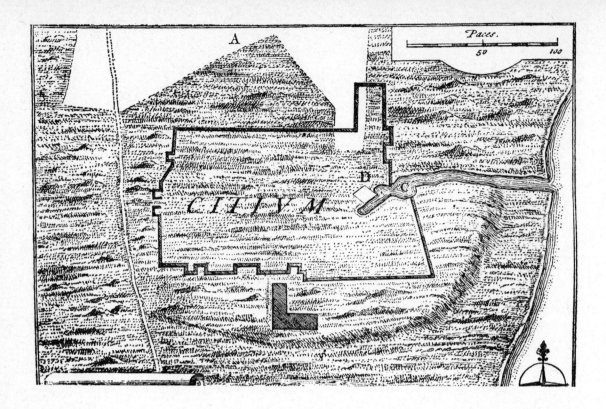

3, 4 *Plans by Pococke (3) and Mariti (4) showing the city wall and harbour of Kition as seen in the eighteenth century*

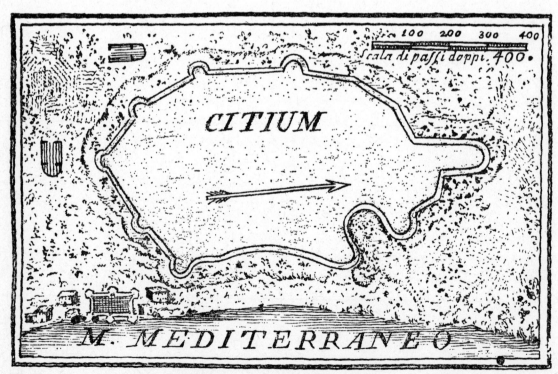

occupied by a small settlement and a cemetery or whether it was only used as a cemetery for settlers across the marshes, or whether there was a strip of land across the marshes through which it communicated with the shore to the west or to the south. It is tempting to suggest that, as in Ancient Egypt, we have here a burial ground where the dead were transported on small boats. Indeed during the Early Bronze Age and probably later such boats must have been very frequently used in order to communicate not only with the islet of Ayios Prodromos but also with the various 'coastal' parts of the ancient town.

The discovery of a few Middle Bronze Age sherds near the Acropolis in 1947 suggested a continuity from the Early to the Middle Bronze Age. It was obvious that in the area of Kition round the Acropolis or north of it near the 'islet' of Ayios Prodromos, there must have been one or more Early Bronze Age settlements of which no architectural remains could, however, be traced. Such settlements, together with their cemeteries, existed in abundance along the south coast and there were more cemeteries for which no settlements had been traced. In the Middle Bronze Age the area lost much of its importance. The copper mines of Kalavassos may justify a development of the south coast during the Early Bronze Age, though this cannot be compared with the greater importance of the northern coast.

This, then, was the information available for the earliest history of Kition and its surroundings. More was known about the later periods both through excavation and through epigraphic and numismatic evidence and we even knew about the very end of the Phoenician town: its last king, Pumiathon, was killed by Ptolemy I in 312 BC and Kition ceased to be an independent town.

II Early Bronze Age Cemeteries at Kition

Fig. 5

Two sites have so far produced Early Bronze Age tombs in the area of Kition – the islet of Ayios Prodromos, mentioned in the previous chapter, and the northern part of the city site of Kition itself. At the site of Ayios Prodromos four large chamber-tombs have already been excavated. The chambers were dug in soft clayish rock; they had a very short and shallow dromos, with the stomion at a much higher level than the floor. The tombs were found half-looted; they contained gifts consisting mainly of Red Polished III ware pottery, mostly with a plain surface, but there were also a few juglets with incised decoration. Large shallow bowls with a conical body were quite common. The fabric and the shapes of these vases recall pottery known from the Early Bronze Age cemetery of Kalavassos, a site near the south coast, west of Kition. They form a regional school with pottery quite distinct from that known from cemeteries along the northern coast. Very few bronze tools were found.

The second site with Early Bronze Age tombs lies within the boundaries of the walled city of Kition. This site, as we shall see, forms a kind of a plateau about 2 m higher than the present-day level of the once marshy land which must have been washed in antiquity by the shallow waters of the marshes. Along the northern slope of this plateau, just below the Late Bronze Age city wall which followed its ridge, a series of five chambers was found dug in soft clayish rock; all of them had been looted, but several Red Polished III ware sherds and even complete vases were enough to date them to the Early Bronze Age. Three chambers containing Early Bronze Age material were found at a distance of about 10 m to the south, *intra muros*, dug on the flat surface of the plateau itself. They had no dromos, or a very short and shallow one, like the chambers of the tombs of Ayios Prodromos. No doubt this shape was dictated by the

Plate 1

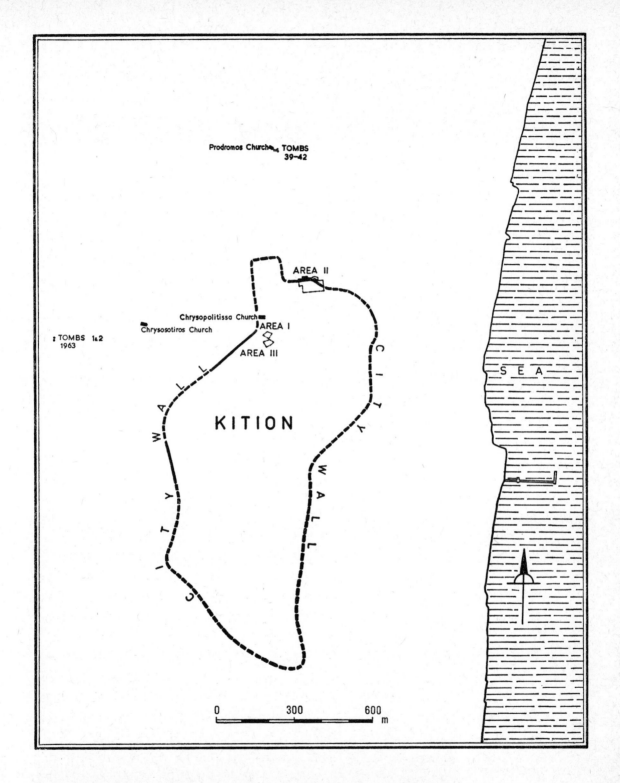

Prodromos Church TOMBS
39–42

Chrysopolitissa Church
Chrysosotiros Church
AREA I

TOMBS 1&2
1963

AREA II

AREA III

KITION

C
I
T
Y

W
A
L
L

C
I
T
Y

W
A
L
L

SEA

0   300   600
                              m

5   Plan showing the city wall (continuous lines indicate parts of the city wall already uncovered, the dotted line is hypothetical); in the northern part Areas I, II and III have been excavated. North of Kition lies the Early Bronze Age cemetery of Ayios Prodromos

Plate I

softness of the clayish rock. The material collected from these tombs consisted of pottery not unlike that of the tombs of Ayios Prodromos. Three more tombs (6, 7 and 8) were found farther south in Area I. Two of them (6 and 8) contained rich ceramic material, including a high percentage of small Red Polished III–IV ware or Black Polished ware vases decorated with incised patterns. It is strange that apart from very few small bronze implements found in the tombs of Ayios Prodromos, none was found in the other Early Bronze Age tombs of Kition. We know that tombs of this period usually contain quite a lot of bronzes and there is no reason why the Kition tombs should be an exception. Almost all the tombs were disturbed in antiquity, though the pottery was not removed. When the Late Bronze Age town was built on the site of the cemetery in Area II, the newcomers may have robbed the tombs which they must have encountered in the foundations of their houses, of all their bronze tools or weapons – still useable if only as scrap metal. A comparable phenomenon occurred at the same site, as will be seen below, towards the end of the thirteenth century B C when newcomers robbed the early and middle thirteenth-century tombs of all their gold objects. The tombs of the Early Bronze Age excavated in the area of Kition so far may date to *c.* 1800 B C.[23]

As already stated, no traces of an Early Bronze Age settlement have been found anywhere at the site. It is possible that there may be other small settlements, one of which may lie on the same site as the Late Bronze Age town. In this case it is unlikely that any undisturbed walls or floors would have been found, since the Late Bronze Age inhabitants of Kition had levelled the ground, as far as present evidence shows, in order to build their own town. The frequent occurrence of Early Bronze Age sherd material between the earliest floor of the Late Bronze Age buildings and the bedrock in Area II favours this hypothesis.

A few Middle Bronze Age sherds were found lying on the bedrock in Area II. As in the case of Early Bronze Age sherds it is not easy to determine whether they come from tombs, looted in antiquity, or from the floors of habitations; whatever the circumstances they bear witness to the continuation of the occupation of the site down to the Middle Bronze Age. After that there is a period of about 400 years which is not yet represented archaeologically at Kition. It is probable that the site may have been abandoned and that the population shifted to the south-west, to the new town which started emerging on the west bank of the Salt Lake with its well-protected inner harbour. This was already a flourishing town in the sixteenth century BC, as we know from the wealth of the tombs excavated in the late nineteenth century. This may be the same phenomenon as on the east coast, where the important Middle Bronze Age settlement of Kalopsidha was succeeded in the seventeenth century BC by the harbour town of Enkomi which was destined to become one of the most important towns of Cyprus in the Late Bronze Age. It is at this period, round the seventeenth century BC, that the Cypriots may have begun to develop their maritime awareness and build coastal harbour towns to trade with neighbouring countries.

III The Earliest Town of Kition and its Tombs

Fig. 6

Fig. 7

In 1959 in a small building-plot near the northern outskirts of the modern town of Larnaca, near the Church of Panayia Chrysopolitissa (Our Lady of the Golden City), a few Late Bronze Age sherds were collected from foundation pits dug for the building of a house. An emergency excavation was undertaken which brought to light two tombs of the thirteenth and twelfth centuries BC respectively, as well as a tomb of the Classical period. Further excavation in an adjacent building-plot in 1962 and 1963 revealed architectural remains of the Late Bronze Age and thus the town of Kition could be safely dated back in the beginning of the thirteenth century BC. This is Area I, to which reference will often be made in the present book. It was obvious, however, that a large open area would have to be excavated, as Area I was unfortunately within the heart of an inhabited quarter, surrounded by houses. After a surface survey of the neighbourhood we discovered at the northernmost limits of the town, in an uninhabited area adjoining the marshy land known as 'Kathari', a row of four large projecting stones, which we suspected of forming part of the city wall. This is the area to which excavations from 1963 onwards have been confined and which we have labelled Area II.

The earliest architectural remains discovered in Area I consist of scanty walls, about 75 cm thick, of which only one course of stones from the foundations survives. The walls form a rectangular room 6 m long and 3·50 m wide, on the hard floor of which, 3·45 m below the present ground surface, quantities of copper slag have been found together with traces of furnaces for copper-smelting. On the northern limits of the building-plot we came upon a portion of a rectangular cemented space, obviously a bathroom floor. No doubt this was an inhabited area associated with material which dates to the thirteenth

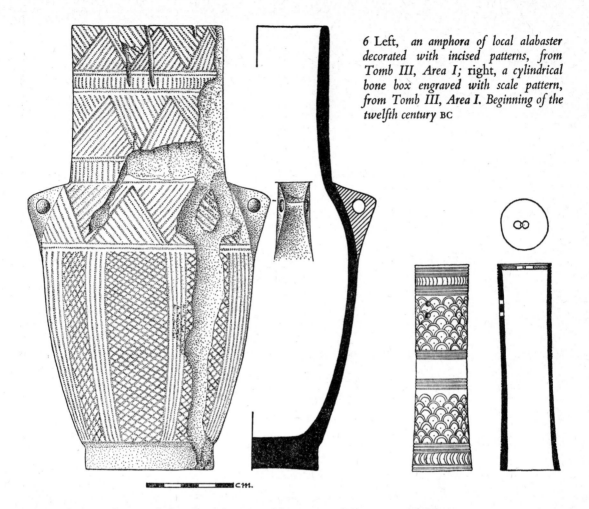

6 Left, *an amphora of local alabaster decorated with incised patterns, from Tomb III, Area I;* right, *a cylindrical bone box engraved with scale pattern, from Tomb III, Area I. Beginning of the twelfth century* BC

century BC. All round the first-mentioned rectangular room, which may be called a workshop, six chamber-tombs were found. Of these, Tombs 6, 7 and 8 are dated to the Early Bronze Age and are referred to in Chapter II. The other tombs – 4, 5 and 9 – are Late Bronze Age in date, contemporary with the thirteenth-century workshop, as we shall see below. This is not a strange phenomenon in Cyprus. It is attested at the Late Bronze Age town of Enkomi, where chamber-tombs have been found in the courtyards of houses; there was no separate necropolis. The same phenomenon is also observed in the town of Ugarit on the Syrian coast.[24]

Tombs 4 and 5 had a common rectangular dromos with both chambers on either side of it on the same axis. The chambers had been disturbed in antiquity. There was quite a lot of pottery in

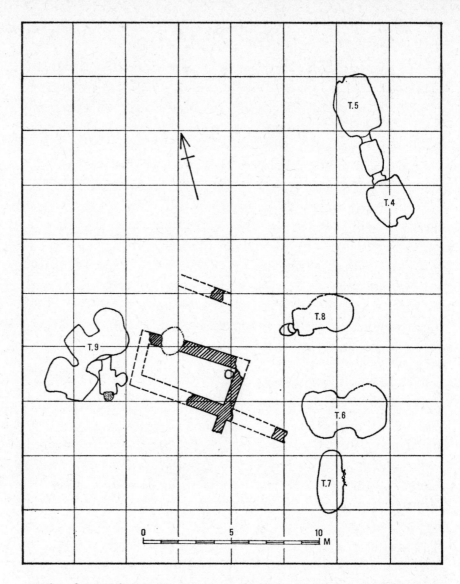

7   Plan of Area I showing Late Bronze Age buildings and chamber-tombs of the Early Bronze Age (Tombs 6–8) and of the Late Bronze Age (Tombs 4, 5 and 9)

both, mostly broken, as well as objects in faience, ivory, alabaster, etc., but not one single object of gold, silver or bronze. Furthermore, sherds which were found in the chamber of Tomb 4 fitted others found in Tomb 5 and vice versa. The dromos, too, was filled with sherds belonging to both tombs. We concluded that at a later period in antiquity (see below) these tombs were discovered and were robbed of all the precious metal objects which they may have contained. Their contents were taken out, searched, and then thrown back indiscriminately into both chambers. This 'disrespect' for the dead is a phenomenon which also occurs in Mycenaean Greece.[25] Tomb 9, however, lying at a distance of about 15 m from Tombs 4 and 5, was found intact, as its roof had collapsed and thus there was a 1·50 m layer of soft clayish rock above the upper layer of contents. Subsequent builders who discovered Tombs 4 and 5 and looted them were deceived by the presence of clayish rock and built on the collapsed roof of the chamber of Tomb 9, mistaking it for the real rock surface and thus leaving the contents of the chamber untouched.

Plate 2

The material from Tombs 4 and 5 has been catalogued together in view of the circumstances of its discovery. The gifts from both tombs total 238, though a considerable number of the objects was found fragmentary or much damaged. Nevertheless they give an accurate picture of the character of the gifts, excluding the absence of metal objects for the reasons stated above. What is immediately striking is the high percentage of Aegean vessels compared with local wares. They constitute almost 35 per cent of all the objects found within the tombs and 38 per cent of the pottery of the tombs. This is indicative of the degree of penetration of Mycenaean culture into Cyprus, whether we accept that Mycenaean pottery was made in Cyprus or in the Peloponnese with the Cypriote market in mind.[26] Of the eighty-six Aegean vases referred to above, nine are Cretan imports and, as we shall see later on, eight such vases came to light in Tomb 9. Considering the scarcity of Late Minoan fabrics in Cyprus this number is important and may justify a special link between Kition and Crete during the thirteenth century BC. This may also be the case at the Late Bronze Age town near the Larnaca Salt Lake (Hala Sultan Tekké), where equally important quantities of Late Minoan vases have been found. What is remarkable is that these Late Minoan vases are not storage jars, like the large stirrup jars known from Enkomi and elsewhere, but cups and other small vases of fine quality. Their clay and fabric resemble remarkably those from the region of Khania in western Crete, where Cypriote White Slip II wares have recently been found. It is probable, therefore, that a special link existed between Kition and Hala Sultan Tekké on the

Plate 3

one hand, and the western part of Crete on the other.[27] The reason
for this contact may have been the trade of copper from Cyprus and
olive oil from Crete, judging from the fairly high number of large
Late Minoan stirrup jars found in Cyprus.

Of the Mycenaean vases there are several with shapes which are
peculiar to the Levantine region: two jugs with cylindrical body,
carinated shoulder and trefoil mouth, two stemmed shallow bowls
with a string-hole handle at the rim, and a lentoid flask. Their ap-
pearance supports the suggestion that they may have been made in
Cyprus by Mycenaean potters.[28] There are eight vases, mostly
fragmentary, decorated with pictorial motifs such as bulls, bull
protomes, octopuses, fishes, birds, etc. Of these a shallow bowl
decorated on the interior with stylized flying swallows should be
noted. The painter who decorated this vase is also known from four
other vases, all bowls, of which two were found in Ugarit, one in
Cyprus and a fourth of unknown provenance.[29] There is another
bowl which is decorated with stylized bull protomes in the same
fashion as the swallows. Of the painter who decorated this vase and
who is known as the 'Protome Painter B', we know four other
bowls, of which one was found in Ugarit, the second of unknown
provenance, the third was found in Tomb 9 at Kition and the fourth
in a tomb at Pyla-Verghi, a few miles east of Kition near the south
coast of Cyprus.[30] Is it accidental that out of five works by the same
painter, three were found in the same area of Cyprus? Or should
we suppose that a Mycenaean painter was working in an atelier of
this region, producing luxury vases for rich clients?

A number of Mycenaean vases bear one or more signs of the
Cypro–Minoan syllabary, engraved or painted after firing. It is still
uncertain what the significance of these signs is, but one may suggest
that they are the initials of a merchant or the owner. Three Mycenaean vases from Tombs 4 and 5 bear an identical group of two such
signs engraved after firing. No doubt the Kitians were a literate
people like the inhabitants of Enkomi and Hala Sultan Tekké.
Though we do not yet have any long texts engraved on tablets, as at
Enkomi, nevertheless the discovery of a number of bone *stili* for
writing on clay suggests that one day such tablets will come to light

Plates 4, 5

Plate II

Plate 6

Plate 7

Plate 8

at Kition. An inscribed clay ball was found in 1973 in the excavations at Hala Sultan Tekké.

Other objects found in Tombs 4 and 5 are of glass, faience, ivory, and Egyptian alabaster. We may also attribute to one of these tombs an object of exquisite beauty, a conical vase (rhyton) of faience, which was found just outside the dromos of the two tombs near Tomb 5 together with other objects which were thrown out of the tomb at the time of its looting. Of no value to the looters, it was disregarded as were all objects of clay, ivory, etc. It is complete except for the vertical handle and tip of the pointed base. Its existing height is 28 cm (originally it may have been 33 cm). It is made of thick, hard faience, covered inside and outside with a thick layer of blue enamel. The outside surface is divided by ridges in relief into three horizontal registers, two of which are decorated with pictorial compositions (upper and middle) and one (lower) with vertical rows of running spirals. They are either painted or inlaid. The upper register contains three galloping animals, two bulls and one goat (or antelope?). The goat and one of the bulls are drawn in black outlines filled with yellow paint, while the second bull is painted in a black outline and is inlaid in dark red enamel. The second register is decorated with two huntsmen and bulls. The first huntsman, wearing a short kilt and a conical tasselled cap, raises his right arm and is ready to strike his victim with a short dagger held in his right hand, while with the left he seizes the animal by the left leg. This attitude is common in Egyptian iconography. The hunter wears what look like winged sandals. Is this a predecessor of the Greek god Hermes, who is also connected with cattle in another way? The second huntsman is almost identical to the first; he holds with both hands the rope which passes round the neck of a bull. In both cases the human figures are rendered in inlaid red enamel and the bulls in yellow paint. There are stylized flowers in yellow paint and red enamel freely scattered against the background, as on Mycenaean vases of the pictorial style. The running spirals of the lower register are in yellow paint. This is an extraordinary work of art, both from the point of view of technique and of decoration. The shape is Aegean as are the running spirals, stylized flowers and the attitudes of some of the

Plate III

galloping animals. The huntsmen, however, are Syrian-looking. A recently published faience lid from Sinai is decorated with a galloping antelope, very similar to the one on the Kition rhyton.[31] Artistically we may consider this vessel as 'Aegeo-Oriental' – a fusion of Aegean, Syrian and Egyptian elements. The style and the technique of the animal decoration recall the Amarna period in Egypt and it is not unlikely that it may have been made earlier than the thirteenth century BC, probably in Cyprus, by an artist who was familiar with fashions which prevailed in Near Eastern art during the fourteenth–thirteenth centuries BC.

Fig. 8

Tomb 9 was found intact for the reasons explained earlier. Its spacious chamber (5·70 m × 3 m), with three large niches on one side, was used for the burial of eleven individuals, of which two were adult males and nine adult females; there were no infants or children. The skulls have been studied by a craniologist[32] and the results of the analysis are of extreme importance. All the individuals had been subjected to at least one form of cranial deformation due to the use of a cradle-board, as is known also from the Neolithic skulls of Khirokitia and sites in the Near East. The deformation of the Kition skulls may be seen in the flattening of one side of the head with the concomitant swelling or bulging out of the other side. This was observed on skulls of both males and females. The deformation occurred while the infant was bound to its cradle-board, not while on its back (as this would be very painful) but while lying on its stomach, with the head turned either to the right or left.

There was a second category of cranial deformation, however, which is far more interesting: some of the skulls had a flattened top. All these skulls belonged to adult females. This kind of deformation was not made as part of a practice of beautification, but, according to the craniologist who studied the details of the other parts of the skulls, was caused by use of the head for carrying or supporting heavy objects. Such phenomena have been observed on skulls of female adults from Hala Sultan Tekké and other Late Bronze Age sites in Cyprus which have been studied at the same time as the Kition skulls. The female adults buried in Tomb 9 were offered exotic gifts and jewellery of great value, indicating that their cranial

1 Chambers of Early Bronze Age tombs along the ridge of the plateau of the northern part of Kition. On the left of the row of chamber tombs is a rectangular bastion; on the right the Cyclopean city wall

2 Detail of the stratification above Tomb 9. Above the surface of the upper burial a thick layer of rock represents the fallen roof; above it is a wall built at the very end of the thirteenth century BC

3 Late Minoan IIIA stirrup jar from Tombs 4 and 5

4,5 Pottery of Mycenaean IIIB ware of specifically Levanto-Mycenaean form from Tombs 4 and 5: (4) a stemmed shallow bowl with string-hole handle; (5) a lentoid flask

6 Shallow Mycenaean IIIB bowl from Tombs 4 and 5, decorated on the inside with stylized bull protomes. A work of the 'Protome Painter B'

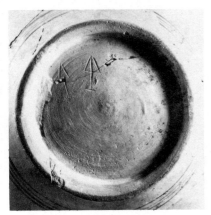
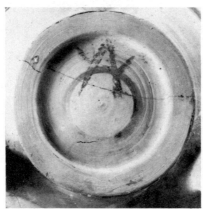

7   Engraved or painted signs of the Cypro-Minoan syllabary were found on both Mycenaean vases and local wares, from Tombs 4 and 5. The examples illustrated here are on Mycenaean IIIB vases. Two of these signs occur on more than one vase

8   Bone stylus from Area I. Such styluses were used to engrave signs on clay tablets before firing. The presence at Kition of such styluses suggests that this site may one day produce tablets of the Cypro-Minoan syllabary such as have been found at Enkomi

9, 10 Views of the upper burial layer of Tomb 9 showing objects and skeletal remains *in situ*

11 View of the lower burial of Tomb 9 showing broken pottery and skeletal remains *in situ*

12 Late Minoan IIIB three-handled jar from the lower burial layer of Tomb 9

13 Kylix of Anatolian origin from the lower burial layer of Tomb 9

14 Mycenaean IIIB jug of a specifically Levanto-Mycenaean form, from the lower burial layer of Tomb 9

15 Mycenaean IIIB kylix decorated
with bulls. A work of the 'Protome
Painter A' from the lower burial layer
of Tomb 9

16 Lentoid flask of faience covered
with blue and yellow enamel. From the
lower burial layer of Tomb 9

17 Fragment of an ivory disc engraved with a lion (only the head survives) and a tree motif. From the lower burial layer of Tomb 9

18 Cylinder seal of haematite and impression. It is decorated in two registers with seated and kneeling human figures, monsters and antithetic sphinxes. Aegeo-Oriental style. From the lower burial layer of Tomb 9

19 Shallow bowl of 'Late Mycenaean IIIB' ware decorated inside with hatched triangles, encircling bands and a spiral at the bottom. From the upper burial layer of Tomb 9

20, 21 Two deep bell-shaped bowls of 'Late Mycenaean IIIB' ware, recalling bowls of the Mycenaean IIIC: 1 style. From the upper burial layer of Tomb 9

22 Gold finger-ring with a bezel in the
form of a ram's head, made of dark blue
paste and set in a gold mounting.
Egyptianizing style. From the upper
burial layer of Tomb 9

23 Necklace with beads of carnelian,
blue and white paste and glass. From the
upper burial layer of Tomb 9

24 Impression from a gold pendant
imitating the form of a cylinder seal,
engraved with a human figure, fish and
two birds. It probably formed part of a
necklace. From the upper burial layer of
Tomb 9 (see also Plate VIII)

25 Bowl of glazed faience; the glaze is now faded but must originally have been blue. The bowl had a lid which was fixed to the two perforated rectangular lugs near the rim. From the upper burial layer of Tomb 9

26 Pyxis of ivory in the form of bath tub. Originally it had a lid fixed to one side of the rim where there is a dowel hole. From the upper burial layer of Tomb 9

27 Bronze mirror with a long narrow tang which was probably fixed in an ivory handle. Such handles have also been found in the tomb. From the upper burial layer of Tomb 9

28 Bronze jug with a vertically ribbed body recalling the Bucchero ware jugs which had metallic prototypes. This is one of the rare specimens of bronze jugs which survive from the Late Bronze Age. From the upper burial layer of Tomb 9

29 Impression of a haematite cylinder seal, engraved with human figures facing each other, monkeys and guilloche patterns arranged in three vertical panels. Egyptianizing style. From the upper burial layer of Tomb 9

30 Detail of the façade of one of the bastions in Area II built against the city wall. Its height is preserved to 2.50 m

31 The hearth-altar of Temple 2, built early in the thirteenth century BC but retained also for subsequent periods

32 Mycenaean IIIB kylix of a type confined to 'Levanto-Mycenaean' pottery. From the earliest floor of Temple 2

33 Fragments of a deep Mycenaean IIIB bowl decorated with human figures (boxers ?) on one side and an octopus on the other. From the earliest floor of Temple 2

34 Fragment of a Mycenaean IIIA (?) crater portraying a female figure with long hair and naked breasts. From the earliest floor of Temple 2

35 Ivory wing of a sphinx with feathers engraved on one side. It probably formed part of a piece of furniture (inlaid with wood) or was the lid of a pyxis. From the earliest floor of Temple 2

36 Detail of the stratification in Area I: in the foreground (right corner) the dromos of a tomb, sealed by a thick layer of clayish soil which represents the floor level of the new buildings, some of them constructed of ashlar blocks, of the end of the thirteenth century BC

37–40 Mycenaean IIIC:1b pottery found in association with buildings of the very end of the thirteenth century BC in Areas I and II. Fragment 39 depicts a bird. Fragment 40 is a bell crater decorated with antithetic spirals on either side of a chequered panel. The commonest shape is the bell-shaped bowl

deformation did not imply an inferior class but that it was a regular practice for Cypriote women, at least during the Late Bronze Age.

Two distinct burial layers have been observed in the tomb, divided from one another by a layer of soil about 10 cm thick. They differ chronologically, the lower being the earlier, but the lapse of time separating the two is only fifteen or twenty years as study of the material shows. The material of the lower burial is strikingly similar to the material of Tombs 4 and 5. Out of 140 objects, eighty-eight are Aegean vases, constituting the very high percentage of 64 per

Plates 9–11

8 *Plan of the chamber of Tomb 9 with its various side chambers. There are two burial layers, separated by a short chronological interval. Eleven individuals were buried in this tomb. The plan shows the upper burial*

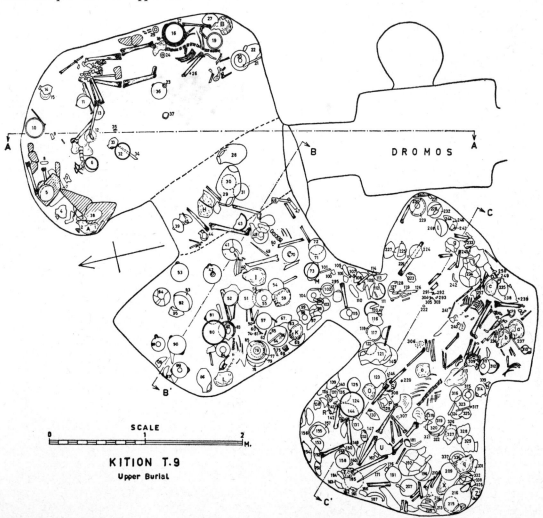

SCALE

KITION T.9
Upper Burial

cent. If we consider that there were 114 vases in all, then the Aegean vases constitute 77 per cent of the total. Of the Aegean vases eight

Plate 12

are Late Minoan, a phenomenon which we discussed above when commenting on the contents of Tombs 4 and 5. There is also another

Plate 13

foreign import, a kylix of Anatolian origin. Two other kylikes of the same fabric have been found, one in a tomb at Hala Sultan Tekké, and another from the recent excavations carried out at the same site by the Swedish Expedition under Professor P. Åström. Considering the scarcity of Anatolian imports to Cyprus during the Late Bronze Age, this new material, along with a crater from the neighbouring site of Pyla-Verghi found in a tomb excavated by P. Dikaios, is significant for relations between Cyprus and Anatolia.[33]

Among the Mycenaean vases two Levantine forms may again be

Plate 14
Plate IV

noted: a jug with cylindrical body, carinated shoulder and trefoil mouth, and a bowl imitating the shape of Cypriote Base-ring ware bowls with a wish-bone handle. There is an extraordinarily high percentage of stemmed kylikes (more than fifteen), which is significant in as much as their scarcity in hitherto known tomb-groups was often commented upon as a peculiarity of the Cypriote taste for specific Mycenaean shapes.[34]

It is unfortunate that the ceramic material is so fragmentary. Nevertheless it helps to reconstruct the fine quality Mycenaean fabrics which were offered as gifts to the dead. These include a number of vases decorated with pictorial motifs such as bulls, octopuses, birds and fishes. Of particular note is a stemmed kylix decorated

Plate 15

with a bull on either side. The kylix may be attributed with certainty to the so-called 'Protome Painter A', of whom nine other works, all found in Cyprus, have been distinguished. One is a fragment of a kylix from Tomb 9. The speciality of this painter is the portrayal of protomes of bulls though he also painted complete bull figures. The bulls, drawn in outline, are filled with cross motifs which give the impression of embroidery.[35] This tomb has also produced a bowl by the 'Protome Painter B' already mentioned in the discussion of the Mycenaean vases from Tombs 4 and 5.

The lower layer of Tomb 9 also contained vases of polychrome

Plate 16

faience, a lentoid flask covered with a layer of blue enamel, and several faience bowls, some with painted pictorial motifs of Egyptian style; there are also fragments of glass bottles. Among the ivories a lid with an engraved decoration of a lion (only the head is preserved) and a tree motif of high quality craftsmanship are worthy of note. In addition there is a gold finger-ring with a bezel decorated with an engraved bird and two signs of the Cypro–Minoan syllabary and a cylinder seal of haematite decorated in two registers with seated or kneeling human figures, mythical monsters and animals. The rendering of the sphinxes betrays Aegean influence.

Plate 17

Plate V

Plate 18

Far more numerous and of a different character are the gifts of the upper burial layer. Out of 353 objects, 180 are vases and 173 miscellaneous objects. Of the 180 vases, 150 are bowls of 'Late Mycenaean style', of local Cypriote manufacture imitating 'true Mycenaean' shapes. There is only one proper Mycenaean vase. Sixteen bowls of 'Late Mycenaean' style were also found in the lower burial, thus indicating that the chronological difference between the two is insignificant. Such bowls have also been found by the Swedish Expedition in the well-known Tomb 18 at Enkomi which is dated to the period just before the arrival of the first Achaean colonists. The evidence of Kition Tomb 9 is even more precise as we shall see later on. Among these shallow bowls of poor fabric, decorated usually with encircling bands and a spiral at the bottom, there is one with four fishes in a horizontal zone inside, in the fashion of the bowl with swallows by the 'Protome Painter B' described from Tombs 4 and 5. There are some other bowls which may be considered copies of the earliest bowls introduced to Cyprus by the Achaean settlers at the very beginning of the last quarter of the thirteenth century BC. Similar ceramic material is known from Enkomi, Kourion and Palaepaphos and is dated to the last quarter of the thirteenth century BC.[36]

Plate II

Plates 20, 21

More important than the pottery are the miscellaneous objects from this upper burial layer. There were forty-two gold objects, mostly diadems with an embossed decoration of linear and floral motifs and in one case of bulls' heads; ear-rings (boat-shaped and in the form of bulls' heads in association with a loop); beads from necklaces and finger-rings of various shapes. One finger-ring, decorated with a loose bezel in the form of a ram's head, recalls Egyptian

Plate VI
Plate VII

Plate 22

Plate V
Plates 24, VIII

Plates 23, IX
Plate 25

Plate 26

Plate 28

Plate 27

Plate 29

jewellery; others consist of adjoining chains of loop-in-loop gold wire. Another finger-ring has a bezel which is decorated with an engraved bull marching among tree motifs. A rare gold pendant imitates the shape of a cylinder seal and is engraved in a naïve style with a human figure, a fish and two birds. Among the gold objects there is also a finger-ring with an iron wire round the middle – the earliest occurrence of this metal in Cyprus. Iron must have been considered a precious metal during this period and was only used in the manufacture of tools and weapons about one century later. The use of iron for jewellery is likewise known in the Aegean.[37] In addition there are necklace beads of faience and carnelian, and vases of glazed faience, probably imported from Egypt, either directly or via Syria.[38]

An impressive number of ivory objects indicate the wealth of the Kitians as well as their taste for luxury and exotic goods. Among them may be mentioned two fragmentary mirror handles with engraved patterns, such as those found at Enkomi and Palaepaphos and a pyxis (lid missing) in the form of a bath tub, of fine workmanship. A number of alabaster vases (both imported and local), mortars and pestles of basalt or andesite, and a fine grey-green bowl of mottled steatite were also found.

Sixty-two bronze objects, mostly hemispherical bowls, were found in the tomb along with *phialae* and a jug with vertical grooves on the body, illustrating the prototype of the clay Bucchero jugs. Three bronze mirrors have been found as well as a number of daggers and spear-heads. This clearly indicates the great development of bronze-work in Cyprus towards the end of the thirteenth century BC, even before the arrival of the Achaean colonists. Finally, four scarabs and a haematite cylinder seal with human figures and monkeys taken from Egyptian iconography may be mentioned.

One of the Late Mycenaean IIIB shallow bowls from the upper burial layer of Tomb 9 contained bird bones which have been analyzed and identified as those of a three weeks' old rock dove, evidently placed there as food for one of the deceased.[39]

The contents of Tombs 4 and 5 and Tomb 9 have been enumerated in some detail because they have a direct bearing on the foreign relations of Kition and the social and economic conditions of the

Kitians. The extraordinarily high proportion of Mycenaean and Late Minoan ware, including forms of a Levantine character, present a new element in the discussion of the origin of the Mycenaean pottery found in Cyprus. The Anatolian kylix, faience and alabaster vases, jewellery and seals of an Egyptianizing style, illustrate the foreign relations of Kition. Contacts must have been quite close with Egypt, considering the short distance from the south coast to the Nile Delta. Kition may have exported copper to Egypt, since copper-smelting was practised in the town as early as the beginning of the thirteenth century, as noted above. The amount of gold objects found in Tomb 9 is extraordinary. There are several legends concerning the discovery of gold objects by tomb-looters in the past, and these may be reflected in the name of 'Chrysopolitissa' given to the Virgin Mary (Our Lady of the Golden City), to whom the present church built a few metres distant from Area I is dedicated.

The architectural development of Kition may be followed more clearly in Area II where a portion of the city wall as well as public buildings and workshops have been uncovered. The earliest remains in this area date to the thirteenth century BC and, according to stratigraphical evidence, are not earlier than 1300 BC. This early town was fortified from the very beginning with a wall which followed the ridge of a low plateau of soft clayish rock, washed at the northern part by the marshes. The city wall of Kition had, therefore, a very irregular oblong shape dictated by the formation of the ground whose abrupt edge offered additional fortification. Very little is known about this early city wall. It has been traced at two localities, in Area II and farther west in an unexcavated area where it can still be seen above ground. It was built of mudbricks, resting on a low course of rubble set directly on the bedrock. In the unexcavated area this wall is preserved to a height of more than 1 m. Two rectangular solid bastions have been found, constructed originally against the mudbrick wall. They are of ashlar blocks at the three exposed sides, while the core was of rubble. The ashlar blocks measure approximately 60 × 40 × 30 cm. The two bastions, separated by a space of 24 m from one another, are of different dimensions: one measures 18·30 m in length and 5 m in depth and is preserved to a height of

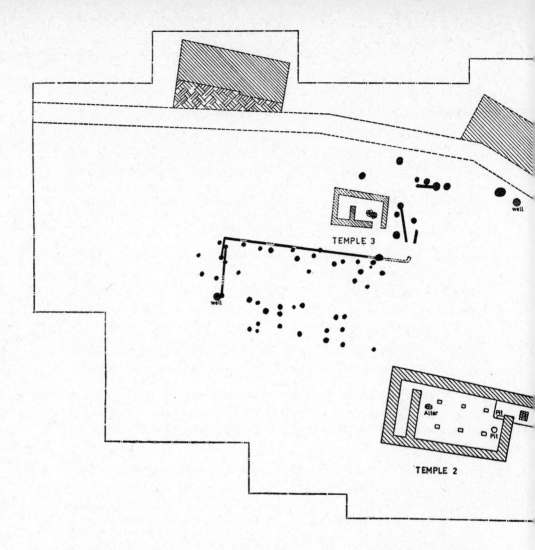

TEMPLE 3

well

well

Altar

Pit

Pit

TEMPLE 2

Plate 30

about 1 m. The second bastion measures 13·50 m in length and 5 m in depth, but is preserved to a height of 2·50 m. Probably their upper parts were of mudbrick. These bastions, built below the level of the top of the plateau, must have been washed in antiquity by the marshes. In fact it was possible to excavate them down to their foundations only during the month of September which is the driest month of the year. In winter the entire height of the bastions is covered by the rising water and this must also have been the case in antiquity. Thus an extra defensive element was offered by the water, in the same way as in the fortifications of medieval coastal towns, like Famagusta on the east coast of Cyprus, where the towers of the Venetian walls are built right in the water.

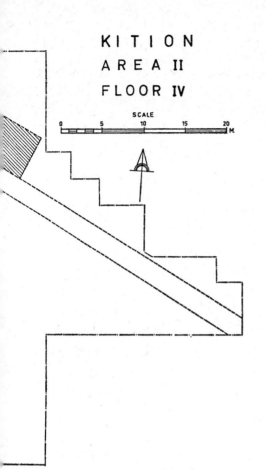

SCALE

0   5   10   15   20
                        M.

9 *Area II: Temples 2 and 3 of the Late Cypriote II period, built early in the thirteenth century* BC. *Between them are pits for sacred gardens. To the north of Temple 3 runs the city wall with its two rectangular bastions*

Intra muros only two structures were found over an area of about 4000 square m. These are two sanctuaries, which we have called Temple 2 and Temple 3, separated by a distance of less than 20 m. Their plan is a standard Near Eastern type, found at Lachish, Tell el-Far'ah and elsewhere, with a courtyard to the east and a narrow holy-of-holies to the west, separated by a parapet wall from the courtyard.[40] In front of this wall inside the courtyard is a hearth-altar.

Temple 2 is the largest. Its foundations were of rubble stone but the walls may have been of mudbrick. Its total length is 14·50 m and its width *c.* 9 m. The narrow corridor of the holy-of-holies measures 2·40 m. There was a lateral entrance to the courtyard in the north-east corner, with a threshold elevated 10 cm above the floor. There

Fig. 9

Plate 31

Plate 32

Plate 33
Plate 34

Plate 35

Plate X

was also a lateral entrance to the holy-of-holies on the same axis as the entrance to the courtyard. Two rows of pillars in the courtyard supported two porticos, along the north and the south walls of the courtyard respectively. The six rectangular bases of the pillars, which may have been of wood, have been found *in situ*. The hearth-altar lies outside the roofed porticos so that the smoke from sacrifices could go out to the open. On the grey-clayish floor of the courtyard, which lies directly on bedrock, enough pottery has been discovered to date the sanctuary to the thirteenth century B C.

Apart from local wares some fine Mycenaean wares have been found, including a handleless chalice with a long stem and a carinated body, a type which is peculiar to the 'Levanto–Mycenaean' class of pottery. Such chalices have been found in other Late Bronze Age temples in the Near East.[41] There were also two fragments with a pictorial representation: one showing a human figure (a boxer?) and an octopus, and the other the upper part of the figure of a woman with naked breasts and long locks of hair. There were also fragments of polychrome faience vases, faience beads, the flat ivory wing of a sphinx(?) decorated with engraved patterns – obviously the lid of a pyxis or even part of the inlaid decoration of a piece of furniture.[42] The most interesting find is a small flat piece of bronze, 4·1 cm long, 2·8 cm wide, and 0·9 cm thick. It is kidney-shaped and has on one side two engraved signs of the Cypro–Minoan syllabary and a vertical bar.[43] The same inscription also appears on votive bronze ingots found at Enkomi, a fact which helps to identify this object as a votive kidney and to interpret it on the analogy of the clay votive livers found in thirteenth-century layers at Hazor and Ugarit. These also bear inscriptions and were used by priests practising divination to teach apprentices. There were also short inscriptions, probably commemorating a sacrifice or a ceremony.

Temple 3 is constructed of rubble at its foundations and the superstructure was probably of mudbricks; it measures 6·75 m in length and 4·15 m in width. It is of more or less the same plan as Temple 2 but has no pillars in the courtyard, to which there is a lateral entrance at the south-east corner with a lateral entrance to the holy-of-holies in the northern part.

We believe that these two sanctuaries, so close together, were used as twin sanctuaries like those which appear elsewhere in the Near East, as for example at Beisan (Temples 4 and 5), at Beycesultan and Boghazköy in Anatolia and probably in the Aegean.[44]

There were no traces of any structures round the temples and moreover none in the whole of Area II so far excavated. Bedrock was reached in the space around and between the two temples and a number of pits were found, about sixty in all, dug into the soft bedrock. Their average diameter is 30 cm and their average depth 50 cm. Some are connected with channels and are associated with two water-wells. The pits may have been used to plant small bushes or flowers for a sacred garden and were connected with ritual ceremonies in the temples. Such gardens are known in Egypt during the XVIII and the XIX Dynasties.[45] In Cyprus they are the first to be discovered so far, but others must have existed at Paphos in the temple of Aphrodite. In the Classical period we know that Aphrodite was worshipped at a locality called Ἱεροκηπίς or Ἱεροκηπία, meaning 'the sacred garden'.[46] The sacred gardens of Kition may be the oldest yet found in the Mediterranean region, though the existence of sacred trees is known at the Late Bronze Age temenos of Ayia Irini on the north-western coast of Cyprus.[47]

The area uncovered is relatively small and no doubt other structures will come to light, contemporary with the two sanctuaries, when the excavation is extended. Already the presence of quantities of copper slag in stratified layers, which also contained Mycenaean pottery (beginning of the thirteenth century), warrant the presence of workshops for the smelting of copper somewhere in the vicinity – predecessors of the twelfth-century workshops to be described in Chapter IV.

IV The Arrival of the Achaeans

Life in the prosperous town of the early thirteenth century BC, from which a few architectural remains and three tombs have been described, suddenly came to an end. The few remaining walls show no signs of violent destruction. The wealth of the upper burial layer of Tomb 9, dated to the last quarter of the thirteenth century, does not suggest a period of gradual decline but rather one of considerable wealth, the result of brisk trade with the Aegean and the Near East. The derelict walls of buildings and the abandoned floor of the workshop in Area I may suggest an abandonment. The reason for this may have been a calamity caused by a natural phenomenon, possibly a drought which led to a temporary departure of the population. This theory has been proposed by several scholars for the Aegean and Ras Shamra and may be valid for Kition and indeed Enkomi and the other Late Bronze Age towns of Cyprus.[48] In Greece, however, this drought may have lasted longer. Achaeans from the Peloponnese left their houses at Mycenae and Pylos and departed as refugees to the Eastern Mediterranean. It is during this period that we may place the events to which there are allusions in the myths of the Trojan war, namely the foundation of towns in Cyprus by Greek heroes at the end of the war. This is supported by archaeological evidence both at Enkomi and at Kition which from now on have the same cultural development and are affected by the same events.

Plate 36

In **Area I** at Kition a thick layer of clayish soil, often about 20–30 cm thick, was spread over the entire area, covering the foundations and floors of buildings of the previous phase. It is upon this later ground level that new houses were built, following a completely new conception of town planning and style in architecture. This would suggest the arrival of a new population, probably accompanied by the old stock who came back to their native land. The introduction of new architectural conceptions and a kind of pottery which was hitherto alien to Cyprus supports this. The pottery, which almost entirely ousted the old local fabrics, is stylistically similar to that in use in the Aegean, particularly the Peloponnese, towards the end of the thirteenth century B C. It is legitimate, therefore, to suggest that these newcomers were Achaean Greeks from the Peloponnese. In building their new houses they must have come across the tombs in the courtyards of the old abandoned houses. These they robbed of their valuable objects, as in the case of Tombs 4 and 5. Only the contents of Tomb 9 escaped their notice because of its collapsed roof which deceived them. The period which elapsed from the time of the abandonment of the town to the arrival of the Achaeans must have been less than twenty years, but in any case long enough for the former town to fall into ruins. The pottery in the upper layer of Tomb 9 dates to the very beginning of the last quarter of the thirteenth century B C. The so-called Mycenaean IIIC:1b pottery found on the floors of the houses of the Achaean population dates to just before the end of the thirteenth century B C. Exactly the same phenomenon occurs at Enkomi, where Tomb 18 (Swedish Expedition), containing pottery identical with that of the upper layer of Tomb 9, was found under the floor of the Achaean building known as 'Bâtiment 18' (French Expedition).

Plate 37–40

The limited space of Area I does not allow an adequate study of these architectural features, though in the few rooms of those houses uncovered one can see the new styles in construction. The walls are thicker and better made. In the case of one room the walls are built of river stones up to 1 m whilst the upper part is built of well-dressed ashlar blocks of hard limestone, in the same fashion as the buildings at Enkomi which are associated with the arrival of the Achaeans.

Plate 41

In **Area II** the changes are more dramatic. On the fallen mudbricks of the old city wall a new Cyclopean wall was built in the same style as the city walls of Enkomi, Sinda in the central part of the island and Palaeokastro Maa on the west coast.[49] The solid rectangular stone bastions of the former wall were retained. A stretch of 98 m of this new wall has now been uncovered. Its foundations are constructed of two rows of large stones, those at the inner face being

Plate XI

Fig. 10

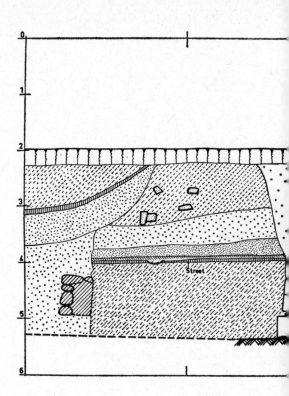

10 *Section showing the foundation of the city wall (right) with mudbricks above it. Against the city wall is constructed a rectangular bastion (centre) with a street running along it (left)*

smaller. The total thickness is 2·40 m throughout. Occasionally there are two large stones, one on top of the other, but in the inner face there is only one, with smaller stones above the larger ones of the lower course, thus forming an inner façade of rubble to a height of 1·25 m. In one area there are three courses of mudbricks above the height of 1·25 m, thus indicating that the superstructure of the wall was of sun-dried bricks, as were the walls of Enkomi and other Near Eastern towns. Instead of large stones occasionally enormous stone anchors are found as building material for the Cyclopean wall. They were probably votive anchors from the sacred area of the sanctuaries of the previous phase.[50] Several dozens of such stone anchors, of various sizes and all used as building material, have been found in Area II. One in the city wall measures 1·30 m × 1·07 m × 32 cm.

The area outside the city wall, between the two rectangular bastions described earlier, slopes down and is covered with a layer of red soil. Part of a street has been uncovered running along the façade of one of the two bastions, probably leading to a city gate to the

Plate 42

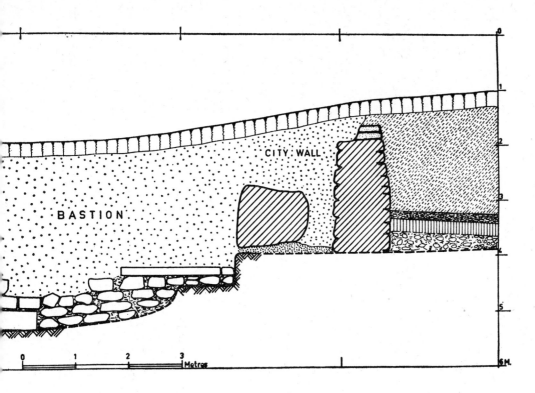

CITY WALL

BASTION

0 1 2 3 Metres

west at a point where the line of the city wall, still unexcavated, turns at right-angles, as can be seen from the surface. This street was constructed on the fallen mudbricks of the earlier city wall. Its surface was very hard, mixed with gravel and quantities of fragments of bones – a phenomenon which occurs also in the texture of the material of the streets of Enkomi. The street measures 3 m in width. Its outer (northern) border was lined with large blocks of stone. On the street surface the tracks of the wheels of chariots and other vehicles were very distinct at the time of excavation.

The site of the two temples of the previous phase retained its sacred character, but the newcomers altered it considerably. The small building of Temple 3 was replaced by a spacious temple numbered Temple 1, and the area between the northern wall of this temple and the city wall, including the site of Temple 3, was levelled up and part of it (on the east) formed an open-air courtyard which we have called Temenos A. The western part, as we shall see below, was used as an industrial quarter. Temple 2 was retained but

Fig. 11

Plate 43

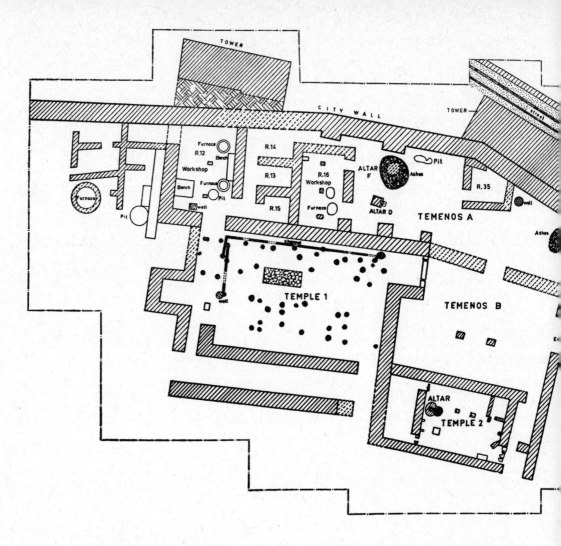

underwent several minor changes in its plan. The space between the
eastern façade of Temple 1 and the north wall of Temple 2, which
join almost at right-angles, was squared off to form another open
court yard, Temenos B. Thus a new sacred area was created, with
twin temples and twin sacred courtyards.

Temple 1 is built on a slight elevation of the ground along the
city wall. It is a rectangular building, measuring *c.* 33·60 m east–west
and 22 m north–south. It consists of a rectangular courtyard with a
small rectangular recess on the western side, 5·30 m in depth and
5·25 m in width. This was probably roofed over and the image of
the deity was probably kept there; this was obviously the holy-of-
holies. There were three lateral entrances to the courtyard, one at the

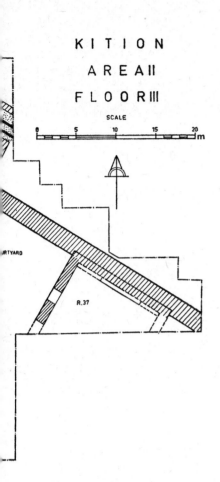

KITION
AREA II
FLOOR III

SCALE

0   5   10   15   20
━━━━━━━━━━━━━━━━━━━━ m

COURTYARD

R.37

11 *Plan of the excavated remains of Area II showing buildings and other features associated with floor III. End of the thirteenth century* BC

north-east corner with a kind of a propylaeum, and two in each extremity of the south side. Along the south wall lay a parallel wall forming a corridor, 3·30 m wide, which was probably roofed and may have served for ceremonial processions. The foundations of the new temple were of large irregular blocks of stone but with a flat top to receive large well-dressed ashlar blocks of hard limestone, drafted along three edges on one side, which formed the inner façade of the courtyard of the temple. Some of these are 3 m long and they are 1 m high. Similar drafted ashlar blocks were used in the construction of public buildings at Enkomi during the same period. Such constructions are also known from Ras Shamra. The outer face of these walls, however, consisted of large stones of irregular

Fig. 12

shape and the core was filled with rubble. This is quite clear in the case of the north wall of the courtyard of the temple which did not undergo later alterations. The rough outer face was unimportant as the courtyard was meant to be seen from the inside where the worshippers stood. The propylaeum was entirely built of large ashlar blocks and had a floor paved with stone slabs. One of the large paving slabs is still *in situ* along its northern side with a rectangular socket through it which might have held a pole for a standard of some kind, like those known from Egyptian or even Minoan temples. The thickness of the walls (i.e. the north wall which retained its original character) was 1·65 m. The western part of the courtyard including the holy-of-holies, was remodelled at a later period and the walls are not in their original form. Of the south wall of the courtyard (not the south wall of the corridor) only the foundation is preserved as this wall was removed at a later period.

The construction of Temple 1 disturbed part of the sacred garden which lay between Temples 2 and 3 of the previous phase, but the main part of the garden was maintained, mostly within the courtyard of Temple 1. The irrigation of the garden had to be modified also since the north wall of Temple 1 was built across one of the irrigation channels. Irrigation of the new garden in the courtyard of Temple 1 was carried out from the well situated in front of the holy-of-holies. There is a channel, running northwards from the well,

Plate XII

I   Red Polished ware from the Early Bronze Age tombs of Area I: amphora, spouted bowl, jug with long neck and beak-shaped spout, miniature juglet supported on three short legs

II   *Left*, shallow Mycenaean IIIB bowl decorated inside with a frieze of stylized swallows, from Tombs 4 and 5. A work of the 'Painter of the swallows'; *right*, shallow bowl of 'Late Mycenaean IIIB' ware, decorated inside with latticed lozenges, a frieze of fishes and a central spiral, from the upper burial layer of Tomb 9

III   Conical rhyton of thick hard faience, covered with a thick layer of blue enamel. The surface is decorated in three registers with galloping animals, bull hunting and vertically arranged running spirals. The various motifs are rendered in black, yellow and green paint and in red inlaid enamel. It was found outside Tomb 5. It is Aegeo–Oriental in style and dates to the thirteenth century BC

I

II

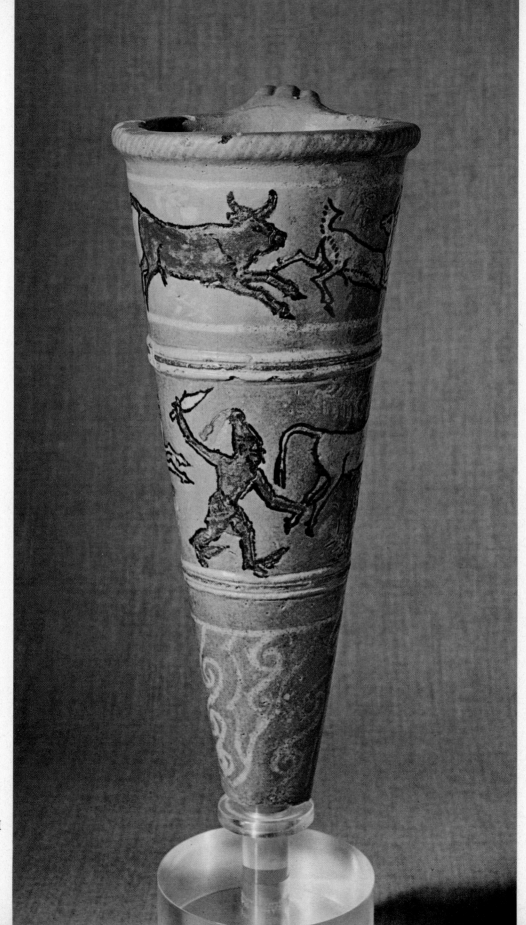

which turns at right-angles to run along the north wall of the courtyard. The holes for bushes or flowers are not in straight lines but
are rather irregularly distributed all over the courtyard. It is difficult
to say, however, whether all of them existed during the previous
phase or whether some were dug for the new temple. Almost in the
middle of the courtyard but nearer to the north wall there is a rectangular pool, measuring 4·60 m in length, 1·80 m in width and
90 cm in depth. It was carved in the bedrock and its bottom was
covered with pebbles. There is no doubt that this pool formed part
of the sacred garden, probably as an ornamental pool or for keeping
sacred fishes, or even for lustral purposes. Such pools existed in
Egyptian temples of the XVIII and XIX Dynasties.[51]

Plate 44

In front of the holy-of-holies, next to the well, is a rectangular
depression which may have held a rectangular column. There is a
similar arrangement in front of the rectangular recess forming the
holy-of-holies at the temple of the 'Horned God' at Enkomi which
has a well next to it. It is here that the sacrifices and libations were
offered to the god in front of his image which stood in the holy-of-
holies. There must have been a table of offerings but it has not
survived owing to later use of the courtyard. There are no signs
within the courtyard of any altar for blood sacrifices, but such an altar
existed in the open Temenos A north of the temple. It is not possible
to say how high the walls of the courtyard were, but the existence
of dowel holes along the inner edge at the top of the ashlar blocks
of the lower course indicate at least one more course. One of the
pieces of lead used in the dowel holes for the dry-fixing of the ashlar
blocks has been found. On the upper façade of one of the ashlar
blocks of the east wall there is an engraved inscription of which only
two signs now survive, the rest having been chipped off. One
sign (absent in the Iron Age script) is peculiar to the Cypro-Minoan
script, confirming the Late Bronze Age date of the ashlar blocks.

Plate 45

Temple 2 was rebuilt more or less on the foundations of the
temple of the previous phase. But whereas the previous temple was
not exactly rectangular (the eastern façade being narrower than the
back of the temple), its ground plan is now rectified. Its dimensions
remain the same, 14·50 m east–west and 9 m north–south. Its walls

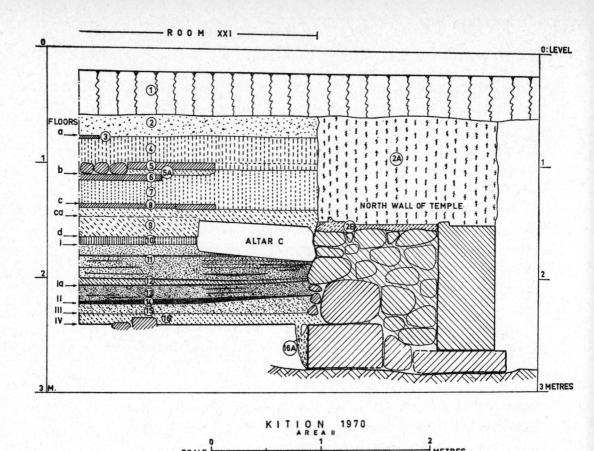

ROOM XXI

0   0:LEVEL

FLOORS

a

1   1

b

c

ca

d

I

2   2

Ia

II

III

IV

3 M.   3 METRES

NORTH WALL OF TEMPLE.

ALTAR C

KITION 1970
AREA II

SCALE   0   1   2   METRES

12   *Section across the north wall of Temple 1 with superimposed layers and floors abutting against its outer face. The inner face is of ashlar blocks*

Plate 46

Plate 47

are built of rubble foundations, but above floor level they are of ashlar blocks of hard limestone, though smaller in size than those of Temple 1. They have drafted edges and a boss in the centre. Of the north wall only the foundations survive because its ashlar blocks were re-used elsewhere during a later period, as we shall see below. The parapet wall which separated the courtyard from the holy-of-holies is built slightly to the east in order to allow more space for the latter structure (3·50 m wide) and is now constructed of ashlar blocks with drafted edges on its outer (eastern) façade, whereas the inner part, which was not seen from the courtyard, was of rubble. A bench was added along the south wall of the courtyard, for the deposit of offerings. Two lateral entrances to the holy-of-holies were now provided, one to the south and the other to the north. The two porticos which existed during the previous phase were reduced to one along the north wall, again supported on three pillars of wood, whose rectangular stone bases have survived; one of them is a fragmentary stone anchor. The entrance to the courtyard was now situated at the south-east corner. It had a threshold of slabs, one of which was a stone anchor. In the north-east corner of the courtyard was a small rectangular enclosure of small stones, utilizing one of the bases of the pillars as a corner stone. This structure lies below the portico and may have been used as a storage space. The hearth-altar of the previous phase was retained, but next to it, to the south, a low table of offerings was constructed.

In front of the east façade of Temple 2 was a parallel wall, built of ashlar blocks, forming a corridor 3·70 m wide communicating with Temenos B to the north of Temple 2. In fact the façade of this parallel wall also formed part of the façade of Temenos B. Thus one could enter Temple 2 from the temenos through this narrow corridor, which may have been roofed as was the corridor along the south side of Temple 1. It is clear that each temple had its own temenos, though the two communicated with each other. Temenos A belonged to Temple 1, while Temenos B was associated with Temple 2.

Temenos A has an oblong, rather irregular shape because its northern boundary, which is the city wall, is not straight but turns at an angle slightly to the south at the point where one of the two bastions is built. Its south wall follows more or less the same line and thus the east part of the temenos is narrower than the western part (maximum width at the western part 11·10 m and minimum width at the eastern part 7·30 m). Its total length is 28 m. At the point where the city wall bends there is a rectangular enclosure, built against the city wall, which may once have been a roofed room within the open courtyard and served as a storeroom. It measures 4·50 m × 4 m. At the western part of the temenos there is a rectangular altar built of ashlar blocks, measuring 1·20 m × 1·20 m; it survives to a height of 60 cm. At its base there is a block of hard limestone carved in the shape of horns of consecration which may once have stood on the top of the altar, as on the monumental altar

Plate 48

69

at the sanctuary of Myrtou-Pigadhes in the north-western part of the island which dates to the same period.[52] The horns of consecration constitute, of course, a symbol of Aegean religion and further attest the identity of the newcomers who rebuilt the sacred complex at the end of the thirteenth century BC. Next to this altar, which may have been of a monumental character or which may have served also as a table of offerings, there is another low altar whose cemented top is slightly above floor level. It has an ovoid shape, with a maximum diameter of 1·50 m, and was found covered with ashes mixed with carbonized animal bones and burnt sherds. Ashes were also spread all round it. There is no doubt that this altar was used for blood sacrifices. Another area of ashes, *c.* 10 cm thick, was found at the eastern extremity of the temenos and may indicate a second place for sacrifices, but this lies directly on the floor of the courtyard with no indication of any altar. Near the south-east corner of the small house referred to above there is a well, whose function within a sacred temenos is obvious.

Plate 49

Temenos B has a roughly rectangular plan; its west wall is the east façade of Temple 1 and its south wall is the north wall of Temple 2. On the northern side it is separated by a wall from Temenos A but its stones were removed at a later date. There is evidence for an opening in the middle of this wall, through which Temenos B communicated with Temenos A. The east wall of Temenos B is a projection of the wall of the corridor in front of Temple 2, which projects to form also the eastern façade of Temenos A. It is built of ashlar blocks of which the lower course survives, but at the north-eastern corner of the temenos there is an orthostat from the second course still *in situ*, 1·18 m high. This must have been a very monumental façade, 23·50 m long and 1·60 m thick, and formed the eastern façade of the sacred complex. In front of it there was an open space, limited to the north by the city wall. It has an irregular shape, narrowing to the south. Its maximum width (northern part) is 11·50 m.

Plate 50

Opposite the façade of the sacred area described above, on the east side of the open space, there is another sacred building (Temple 4).

From this open space, which one may call a 'public square', one could enter the sacred area through a wide door leading to Temenos

B (4·20 m in width); or through a narrower door to the north leading to Temenos A. Though Temenos B is smaller than Temenos A (19·50 m east-west and 12·70 m north-south), it occupies a more central position in the layout of the whole sacred complex. Its monumental entrance is the principal entrance to the sacred area.

Along the south wall of the temenos, on the left-hand side of those who entered through the principal entrance, there are two rectangular blocks of hard limestone, measuring 1 m × 85 cm, which probably were the bases of two columns. It is not impossible that these columns supported a roof for a portico along the south wall of the temenos, recalling the similar architectural arrangement in the sacred area of the Palace of Pylos in the Peloponnese.[53] Two hard limestone capitals which were found nearby may have belonged to these two columns. They have a stepped profile and a square top measuring 1·25 m × 1·25 m and 1·12 m × 1·12 m respectively. Their bottom surfaces are also square, 58 cm × 58 cm in both cases and they are 58 cm and 53 cm respectively in height. Their four sides had three steps each and a 'cavetto' narrowing towards the bottom. A fragment from a third capital was used as building material and a fourth complete capital was chipped on all four sides to provide a base for a column during the Phoenician period. Similar capitals have been found in sanctuaries of the same period (end of the thirteenth century BC) at Enkomi, Myrtou, and recently in the temple of Aphrodite at Palaepaphos. Their origin may be Aegean, though none has been found there yet except for some miniature representations. They may originally have been of wood, as were the columns in Mycenaean architecture, and were copied by the Cypriots in stone.[54]

In the same temenos two blocks of hard limestone have been found, which, when placed together, form horns of consecration of the same type as those found in the open courtyard of the thirteenth-century sanctuary at Myrtou and in the temple of Aphrodite at Palaepaphos. Thus, both Temenos A and Temenos B had altars with horns of consecration, though the actual altar in Temenos B has not survived.

Plate 51

Plate 52

The features described above, i.e. the capitals and the horns of consecration found in various sanctuaries at the end of the thirteenth century in various parts of Cyprus, suggest a homogeneous style in sacred architecture, some features of which were introduced by the Achaean colonists. The sacred architecture of Kition with its monumental ashlar blocks, has already been compared to the temples of Enkomi of the same period. One may ask, however, how this architectural style could have been introduced by the Achaeans, since no examples have so far been found in the Aegean, whereas the nearest parallels are in the Near East, as for example the temple of Baal at Ugarit. The Achaean colonists may have used local talent in building monumental architecture just as their predecessors, the Mycenaeans, profited from contacts with Near Eastern art.

The Industrial Quarter. West of Temenos A, between the north wall of Temple 1 and the city wall, is a row of three consecutive large rooms which, as we shall explain below, were workshops for the smelting of copper. The room on the extreme west, Room 12, measuring 10 m north–south and 7 m east–west, amply attests this function. On floor III, which corresponds with the end of the thirteenth century and is, therefore, contemporary with Temples 1 and 2, remains of channels have been found, as well as fragments of crucibles with copper on the inside walls, fragments of bellows, thick layers of ashes, copper slag and cavities with their walls hardened by fire. There were two such cavities associated with channels and there is no doubt that these were furnaces for smelting. Along the east and west walls of the workshop are two benches with socketed blocks of stones in their corners which imply that they were covered by a shelter. The mineral, probably in a partly processed form, may have been kept under cover on these benches before the final smelting. It must have been crushed on stone slabs, and for this purpose stone anchors were used, still found *in situ*; moreover, several stone pounders were found on the floor of the room. Washing the mineral must have demanded quantities of water. There is a well in an adjacent room; the water was canalized after the washing process to a deep pit in Room 12 which also produced potsherds, dated to the end of the thirteenth century, and copper slag. In all probability Room 12 was unroofed, so that the poisonous fumes from the furnaces could be blown away from the

Plate 54
Plate 53

town by the south wind and thus air-pollution avoided. This may be the reason why here, as well as at Enkomi, the workshops for copper-smelting were constructed near the northern extremity of the town, close to the city wall. It is interesting to note that even in medieval Famagusta metallurgical workshops were built along the northern part of the city wall.

On floor III of Room 12 a circular pit was found, filled with white ashes mixed with tiny pieces of bone. An analysis showed that this was bone ash. In a storeroom west of Room 12 there were similar pits also containing bone ash. In the courtyard of one such store-room was a circular kiln, built of mudbricks, and containing bone ash and carbonized animal bones next to it. According to metallur-gists the mineral of Cyprus is poor in silica and by adding bone ash as fluxing material more metal could be extracted. Here, then, is a real industrial quarter where precious bone ash, so indispensable for smelting, was produced and stored on the spot for convenience.

Plate XIII

Room 12 communicates with its adjacent room to the east, which is divided by parapet walls into three compartments, here labelled Rooms 13, 14 and 15. These compartments communicate with one another through a common corridor which runs in front of them. In Room 14 there was a well, obviously for the needs of the work-shops. Quantities of copper slag have also been found on the floor of this room, as well as traces of furnaces.

Plate XIV

The easternmost storeroom, which is adjacent to Temenos A, is Room 16. It was roofed and had three wooden pillars as roof sup-ports, judging from three stone bases found *in situ*. Traces of fire were found on the floor and on one small furnace or hearth but there were no traces of copper slag. This may be a workshop associated with both the needs of the temples and of the other workshops rather than smelting.

What is surprising, and indeed utterly unexpected, is the proxi-mity of the workshops to the sacred area and, even more so, the fact that they communicate with it. Room 12 communicates directly with Temple 1 through a large opening at the north-western corner of the courtyard of the temple. From Temenos A one could enter workshop 16 through two doorways, and through a narrow passage along the city wall one could go from Temenos A to workshops 13, 14 and 15 and from there to Room 12. This no doubt was not accidental but significant. We believe that metallurgy and religion were connected with each other, as shown below.

In 1963 Professor Schaeffer discovered in a twelfth-century sanctuary at Enkomi the bronze statue of a bearded god, wearing greaves, holding a shield and brandishing a spear, ready to strike. The god stands on a base which takes the form of an oxhide ingot, similar to those which have been found at Enkomi and in the Late Bronze Age shipwreck off Cape Gelidonia. Professor Schaeffer, who published this statue[55] and called it the 'Ingot God', very ingeniously identified it with the god who protects the copper mines of Cyprus. This interpretation received an almost dramatic confirmation by subsequent discoveries. A few years ago a private collector of antiquities at Oxford acquired a bronze statuette of a female deity said to have come from Syria. Its style, however, leaves no doubt about its Cypriote origin. The goddess is nude, and bends her arms below her breasts, in the usual attitude of 'Astarte'. She stands on a base which has the form of an oxhide ingot, and this, of course, brings her directly close to the 'Ingot God' of Enkomi. Dr H. Catling, who published the Oxford statuette,[56] suggested that the goddess may symbolize the fertility of the copper mines and the increase of production in the furnaces. He goes on to suggest that 'the whole of the copper industry in Cyprus may have been temple-based, carried on in the name of the gods to whom the finished products were brought as their due, and on whose behalf the temple property was subsequently either issued to the city's bronzeworkers for the production of manufactured articles or disposed of by internal or foreign trade as surplus in exchange for other commodities'.

We know the importance of Cyprus as a copper-producing country and how flourishing the metal industry was in the island during the thirteenth and twelfth centuries BC. The miniature ingots with inscribed signs in the Cypro–Minoan syllabary found at Enkomi are no doubt votive ingots and may have a religious significance as offerings to the divinities who were worshipped as the patrons of metallurgy. This evidence suggests that during the twelfth century

Plate 55

Plate 56

there existed at Enkomi – and perhaps elsewhere – two divinities, a male and a female, who were worshipped as the protectors of the copper industry of the island which was the backbone of the economy of Cyprus. The discovery at Kition of twin temples associated directly with workshops for copper-smelting emphasizes this and implies that the worship of these two divinities may have been practised in the whole of Cyprus, or at least in all major towns which were connected with metallurgy or the copper trade. This practice at Kition may date to the beginning of the thirteenth century since, as mentioned earlier, quantities of copper slag have been found in Temenos A in layers connected with Mycenaean IIIB pottery, though no traces of workshops from this period have yet come to light.

At Athienou, north of Kition, recent excavations have brought to light a Late Bronze Age sanctuary which produced hundreds of miniature votive vases; in the courtyard of the sanctuary quantities of copper slag have been found. The excavators maintain that this too is a sanctuary dedicated to a god connected with metallurgy as at Kition.[57] The sanctuary may, in fact, have been on the route through which mineral may have been transported from the mines to Kition. A later survival of this practice was discovered not only in the Archaic and Classical temple of Astarte at Kition, as we shall see later on, but also at Tamassos in the central part of Cyprus and near the copper-mining area, where a sanctuary of the Classical period, probably of Astarte, has been found in association with copper-smelting installations. Outside Cyprus, in the southern Arabah, a thirteenth-century sanctuary of Hathor has been found at Timna, situated near copper mines and mining installations.[58] The same goddess was worshipped in Sinai in the sanctuary of the XII Dynasty at Serabit el-Khadem, in a mining area. In Ugaritic mythology we know of Kothar-Khasis, the Smith-god, of the fourteenth century BC,[59] who resembles Hephaestos of Greek mythology. Moreover, round the temple of Hephaestos in the Agora of Athens metallurgical installations dating to the sixth century BC have been found, probably associated with guilds of metalworkers, whose patron god was Hephaestos.[60] Similar practices may be encountered elsewhere: in Anatolia, at Sardis, the Pactolus gold-refining installations are next to a sacred area dating to the seventh–sixth centuries B C, with the altar of Cybele in the middle.[61] It is tempting to see in the two divinities of Late Bronze Age Cyprus the predecessors of Hephaestos and Aphrodite, as the god of metallurgy and goddess of fertility respectively. In any case the discovery of the sacred and the industrial quarters at Kition and their association, as shown above, reveal a new chapter in the religious beliefs of the island during the Late Bronze Age and at the same time emphasize the importance of metallurgy for Cyprus.

We believed that the street and the open courtyard which run along the east façade of Temenos A, Temenos B and Temple 2 marked the limits of the sacred area. At the end of the 1973 campaign, however, part of a fourth temple was uncovered, lying opposite the east façade of Temenos B and along the line of the city wall. This new temple was excavated in 1974.

Fig. 13

Temple 4. Though stone robbers removed the majority of the ashlar blocks of the walls of the earlier periods of this temple, its foundations are sufficiently well preserved to allow a more or less detailed description of its shape and size.

Bedrock was reached only in a looter's pit within the courtyard of the temple which was cleared of its fill, showing in section the surface of the bedrock, and the following superimposed layers: a layer of debris of red mudbricks, covered with a layer of chavara. This must have accumulated above the bedrock when the area along this part of the city wall was levelled and Temples 1 and 2 were constructed as well as the two open courtyards (Temenos A and Temenos B). The debris of red mudbricks no doubt belonged to the superstructure of the Late Cypriote II (early thirteenth century) city wall, which was destroyed and replaced by a Cyclopean wall at the time of the construction of the temples.

Temple 4 faces west, unlike Temples 1 and 2. Its western façade is opposite the façade of Temenos A and Temenos B but not parallel to it. In fact between the two there is an open space, 12 m wide at the northernmost side (along the city wall), narrowing to 8·50 m to the south. This arrangement was no doubt dictated by the direction of the city wall which turns slightly to the south at this point. The north wall of Temple 4 was built against the city wall.

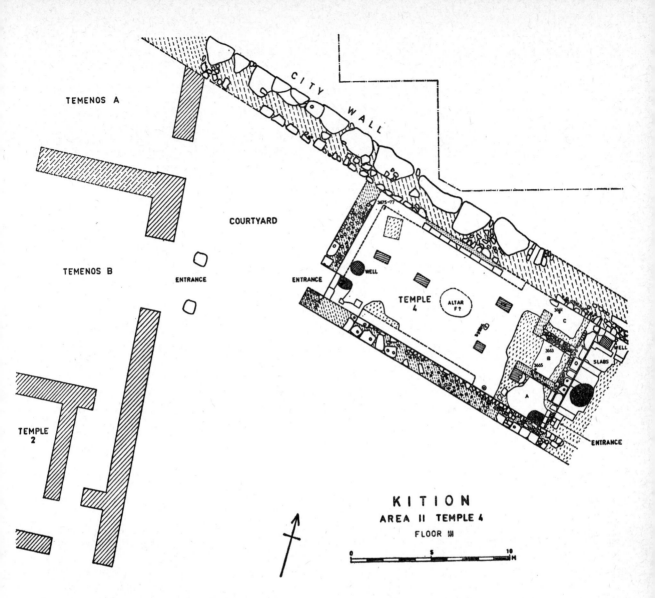

13 *Plan of Temple 4 (floor III) along the city wall, opposite Temene A and B.*
Between the temene lies an open courtyard

In the original phase of the temple, like the other temples so far
discovered in Area II, it was planned and built as a large rectangular
courtyard with a lateral entrance to the west (near the south-west
corner) and two small rooms and an entrance passage adjoining it to
the east. The width of the courtyard is 7·20 m at the western side and
7 m at the eastern side. The total length of the temple, including the
two rooms at the back, is 15·20 m. The width of the temple including

Plate 57

the thickness of the walls is 8·20 m and the length 17·30 m. The two small rectangular rooms at the back of the temple, which may represent the holy-of-holies and which must have once housed the sacred objects, occupy the whole of the east side of the temple. Their floor rises considerably above the level of the floor of the courtyard. Room B forms a rectangular recess on the central axis of the courtyard, without any wall between the two. It measures 1·80 m in width and 2·85 m in length. Room C on the north is screened from the courtyard by a wall leaving a lateral opening for communication with the courtyard. This room measures 2·25 m in length; the width of Room C on the north-eastern corner is 1·80 m. The rectangular space on the south of the central recess of the holy-of-holies (marked as Room A) is a passageway leading from an entrance and threshold at the southern end of the east wall of the temple courtyard, exactly opposite the entrance in the western wall.

As mentioned above, stone robbers took away most of the original ashlar blocks of the temple walls and what remains is only the foundation though some of the blocks survive in the northern wall. There are horizontal ashlar slabs forming a kind of narrow bench along the wall (45 cm wide and 20–22 cm thick). The northern wall of the temple, however, was the city wall itself, the inner façade of which was dressed with thin ashlar slabs, 34 cm high and 18 cm thick. There are very few stones on the wall of the west side of the temple, of which one is an anchor. There are, however, traces of the rectangular slabs, cut in the chavara, which formed the threshold of the entrance. There are also traces of the shallow cavity which held the horizontal ashlar blocks of the bench. The foundations of the south and east walls, about 1 m wide, had their inner face of rubble, whereas the outer face was built of flat stone anchors. The reason for this was no doubt to provide a flat base for the ashlar blocks of the outer face. The same may have been the case for the west wall.

The earliest floor of Temple 4, floor III, was of green clay with very distinct traces of burning. The bench of ashlar slabs, which survives along the north wall, does not seem to have run round the whole perimeter of the courtyard, but only along the middle of the north and south walls and along the west wall.

There are five rectangular bases of hard limestone in the courtyard of floor III, two in the eastern end of the courtyard on a north–south line in front of the holy-of-holies (one under Altar E of floor I, see Fig. 15), and three on an east–west line in the centre of the room. These bases must once have had another smaller rectangular block on top (now missing) which supported a wooden pillar, as far as stratigraphical observation shows. The presence of these three bases suggests a portico along the north side of the courtyard. The function of the other two bases is uncertain. One has a rectangular hole in the middle, probably to receive a wooden pillar. These two column bases are of quite different shape and size. The rectangular hole in the north base indicates that it once held a wooden pillar whereas the south base must have held a stone pilaster. This differentiation strongly suggests that these pillars were not of decorative or architectural but of cultic significance. In the light of this evidence it is very interesting to consider the open air sanctuaries which were very common in early Canaan. They begin in Chalcolithic times (at Ein Gedi) and continue into the Early, Middle and Late Bronze Ages when they begin to influence and be embodied in more substantial temple buildings. This type of sanctuary, called a *Bamah*, featured two forms of cult object: a standing stone, the *Mazzebah*, and a wooden upright, the *Asherah*, which had cultic associations with the sacred Tree of Life. The former represented the male deity and the latter the female. It is quite possible that our pillar bases once held similar images and that twin male and female deities were worshipped in Temple 4 in the Late Bronze Age.[62]

The original altar for floors II and III was never successfully located. The table of offerings for Altar E, which will later be reconstructed on the spot, was removed in order to examine the possibility that the original altar might lie underneath. Instead the easternmost of the north–south line of the three column bases for floors II and III was found. A patch of small stones in the floor in front of the holy-of-holies was also investigated in the search for the missing altar. Although there was some evidence of burning and several bones and Mycenaean IIIC:1b sherds there was no decisive evidence to establish it as the original altar. A well was found at the western part of the courtyard. It contained Mycenaean IIIC:1b sherds as well as a large fragmentary pithos.

Floor III also featured two small pyres – one inside the threshold of the entrance in the western wall and the other on the threshold of the eastern entrance. Both are on the left-hand side as one enters the temple. Each contained large pieces of burnt animal bones and many burnt Mycenaean IIIC:1b sherds.

A number of objects were found on floor III in the holy-of-holies, including several bowls of Base-ring Wheelmade ware, such as those which were found at Enkomi in the temple of the Horned God,[63] a gold ring with an engraved bezel representing a bull and also an ivory handle for an unidentifiable object.

Plate 58

Plate 59

The most important discovery, however, was a cache of three bronze objects lying on top of each other in the north-west corner of the courtyard. They were covered by the deep layer of chavara (18–25 cm thick) below floor III and were lying on mudbrick debris. It is clear that they were placed there deliberately at the time of the construction of floor III and may thus be interpreted as a foundation deposit such as are known mainly from Mesopotamia,[64] but also from Enkomi during the Late Bronze Age.[65] Two of the bronzes are flat T-shaped unfinished tools (ploughshares?),[66] 25 cm long. The third object is a triangular nail or peg 18·3 cm long, with a convex head, measuring 7·5 cm in diameter. The point is rounded; the maximum thickness of this object is 6·5 cm. It was found lying horizontally on the surface of the debris of red mudbricks.

Plate XV

The peg or nail-shaped objects were very popular as foundation deposits in the Near East, particularly in Mesopotamia from the Early Dynastic period onwards.[67] They are found either under the foundations of the walls or under the floor, occasionally in association with ring bolts. Very often they are decorated with figures at the top, but the Kition example is undecorated, with a flat head. The pegs are usually found in a vertical position, in direct contact with the earth; the Kition peg, however, was found lying horizontally on debris of mudbricks. Tablets usually found in association with the foundation deposits or the pegs themselves may bear inscriptions, but none was found at Kition. The two unfinished bronze agricultural tools which appear together with the peg are of types known from other Late Bronze Age sites in Cyprus, either in their unfinished form[68] or as finished tools (ploughshares). It is not easy to say whether these had any specific symbolic meaning or were deposited simply as offerings for their own intrinsic value. The significance of the peg is obvious and it is clear from a Hittite text which refers to the foundation of a temple: 'Just as this copper is secured, (as) moreover it is firm, even so let this temple be secure! Let it be firm upon the dark earth!' The form of the Kition bronze peg is paralleled by a number of clay pegs, usually inscribed, from Mesopotamia.[69]

An area paved with ashlar slabs has been uncovered east of Temple 4 – in fact it abutted directly against the ashlar blocks of the outside face of the east wall of the temple. The central part of this paved area had been severely burnt and in places chavara covers the stones. This may suggest that there was once a kind of an altar on this paved area. The exact size of this area cannot yet be determined because several of the slabs had been removed by robbers and the part in which they are preserved is still to be excavated. There is no doubt, however, that it has a functional relation either with Temple 4 or with another temple. From this area one could enter Temple 4 through its eastern door.

Plate 60

To the north of the paved area there is a square well, constructed with ashlar blocks. Its stomion measures 55 cm × 75 cm; it widens below the stomion to 73 cm × 90 cm. The sides of the well are built of regular horizontal courses of ashlar blocks. The well was dug to a depth of about 5 m when water was reached. Mycenaean IIIC:1b pottery was found in it. This well was constructed as part of the paved area and may have had a sacred significance.

As already noted, from the thirteenth century BC onwards the archaeological and stratigraphical phenomena observed at Kition are paralleled exactly by those at Enkomi. At both sites a major catastrophe, probably an invasion by the 'Peoples of the Sea', destroyed the ashlar block buildings, the sanctuaries and the palaces soon after their construction, in the early part of the twelfth century.[70] But at Enkomi and at Kition reconstruction was rapid and a new town emerged as prosperous as the previous one, at least in the case of Kition.

Fig. 14
Plate 62

The plan of the sacred area and the workshops of the industrial quarter remained more or less the same, but the entrance to Temenos B, which was the principal entrance to the industrial quarter, became a monumental propylaeum, with its side walls measuring 5·40 m in length and constructed with enormous ashlar blocks of hard limestone. A single block of the south side-wall of the propylaeum, the upper part of which was cut away by the stone robbers,

---

IV Mycenaean IIIB bowl imitating the form of Cypriote Base-ring ware bowls with wish-bone handle. From the lower burial layer of Tomb 9

V Gold finger-rings with engraved bezels: *right*, decoration includes a bull (very worn), from floor III of the holy-of-holies of Temple 4; *centre*, a bull walking through bushes or trees, from the upper burial layer of Tomb 9; *left*, a bird and a sign in the Cypro–Minoan syllabary, from the lower burial layer of Tomb 9

VI Gold diadems with embossed decoration, from the upper burial layer of Tomb 9

VII Two pairs of gold ear-rings, from the upper burial layer of Tomb 9: *above*, boat-shaped, with one long end bent over and overlapping the other; *below*, ring with overlapping ends and pendant in the shape of a bull's head with embossed details

VIII Gold pendant imitating the form of a cylinder seal, probably forming part of a necklace. From the upper burial layer of Tomb 9. The impression is shown in Plate 24

IX Necklace beads of carnelian, some of them in the shape of a bottle or poppy. From the upper burial layer of Tomb 9

X Bronze votive kidney with engraved signs in the Cypro–Minoan syllabary on one side, found on the earliest floor of the holy-of-holies of Temple 2. Such votive objects were used by priests who taught apprentices the practice of divination

XI Aerial view of Area II from the west at the end of the 1973 season, showing the excavated part of the city wall and architectural remains

XII Part of the courtyard of Temple 1 near the holy-of-holies, showing pits and irrigation channels; the latter communicate with a well near the entrance to the holy-of-holies

XIII General view of Room 12, showing the bench along the west wall and the pit filled with bone ash, visible in section

IV

V

VI

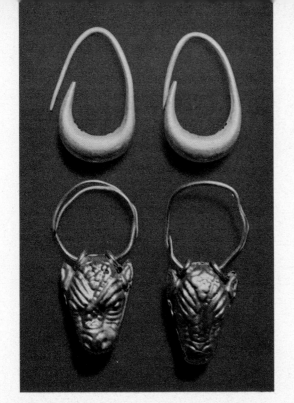

VII

VIII

IX

X

XI

XII

XIII

is 2·25 m long, 1·85 m high and 62 cm thick. No doubt it must have belonged to a construction of the previous period. The floor level of the courtyard of the temenos is raised by one step from the level of the open space to the east of the temenos; underneath the step, at the threshold of the principal entrance, there is a channel through which the rain water from the courtyard was conducted outside into the open space. Though the width of the entrance was slightly reduced, it gained monumentality. The cavities for the door-jambs are still visible, with traces of green corrosion of bronze which suggests that they were metallic. The floors of Temenos A and Temenos B during this second period (all the floors of this phase are labelled floor II; the previous phase corresponds to floor III) were raised and were covered with pebbles. In the north-east corner of Temenos B a square altar was built, measuring 75 cm × 75 cm, lying on the right-hand side for those who entered the temenos through the principal entrance. Quantities of carbonized animal bones and broken vases, all mixed in ashes, have been found all round the altar.

In Temenos A the ovoid altar with the cemented top was covered by floor II, but the rectangular altar with horns of consecration was retained. Patches of ashes on floor II of the temenos suggest that blood sacrifices continued to be practised at the eastern extremity. A revival of the sacred gardens in Temenos A is also evidenced. Eight pits have been found, slightly larger than those inside the courtyard of Temple 1, which may have been intended for bushes or even small trees. The well for the irrigation of the trees and the other needs of the temenos remained in use. There is no evidence of a sacred garden being maintained in the courtyard of Temple 1. Its Late Bronze Age floors were removed during the ninth century BC, as we shall see later on, and no proper stratification may be observed inside the courtyard. Only if the stratification is studied against the outside face of the northern wall of Temple 1 may we perhaps determine its chronological sequence. The workshops continued to function, but only for a short time. The furnace for the roasting of bones to make bone ash was rebuilt above the earlier one and the circular pits of the previous period continued to be used for storing bone ash. Soon, however, the metallurgical installations ceased functioning. The large

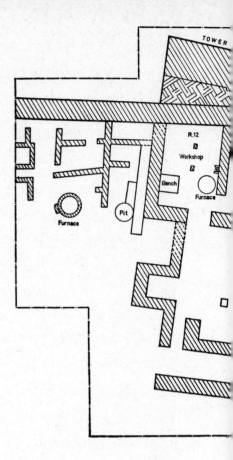

14 *Plan of the architectural developments in the sacred and industrial quarters at floor II*

workshop (Room 12) was roofed as far as one can judge from the two rectangular stone bases for wooden pillars which supported the roof. It is not improbable, however, that the workshop was still used as such if only for bronzework; the actual smelting may have been carried out elsewhere. In this and the adjacent workshops large pithoi have been found as well as quantities of unbaked clay sling bullets lying on the floor. It is not unlikely that at one stage these rooms were used for storing or even for producing sling bullets when the need arose.

In Temple 4, floor II lay immediately above floor III and all the structures and features described above as originating on floor III must be taken as continuing at floor II level. The floors were too close

Plate 61

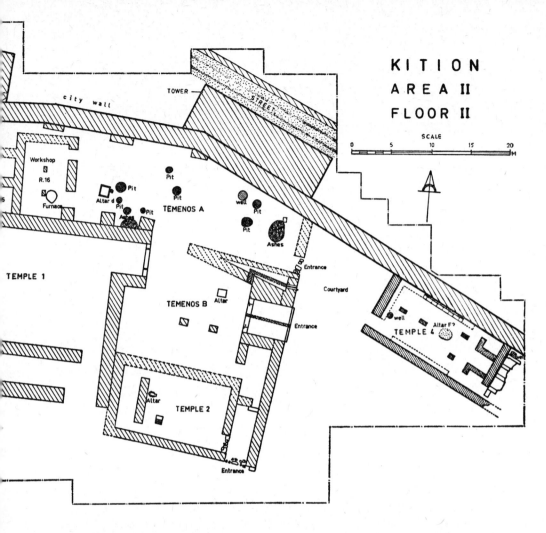

together to allow a feature to be assigned to one and excluded from the other.

No other changes have been observed in Area II. In Area I we noticed the same phenomena but the site is too small for any architectural changes to be observed. The pottery which was found on floor II is of Aegean origin but made in Cyprus. This may attest a new wave of Achaean colonists who reached Cyprus after the catastrophe wrought by the 'Peoples of the Sea'. This phase of floor II, which may be dated approximately from the beginning of the twelfth century to the middle of the eleventh, coincides with the 'Dorian invasion' in Greece after which a new wave of refugees from the Peloponnese may have sought fortune in the Eastern Mediterranean and settled in Cyprus, an island with which they must have kept contact through their kinsmen who emigrated there three generations earlier. The fact that the pottery found on floor II at Kition, as at Enkomi, resembles the pottery discovered in the destruction layers of the granary of the citadel of Mycenae supports this hypothesis of emigration of refugees to Cyprus after the 'Dorian invasion'.[71] Some of these refugees may have been Cretans, considering the various sub-Minoan elements in the so-called 'Proto-White Painted pottery' of Cyprus (end of the twelfth-beginning of the eleventh century BC), quantities of which have been found on floor II at Kition. The relations of the southern coastal towns of Kition and Hala Sultan Tekké with Crete, which, as we have seen, began already in the thirteenth century, were resumed during the subsequent period at Kition.

Plate 63

During the second quarter of the eleventh century BC a physical phenomenon, probably an earthquake, put an end to the Late Bronze Age town of Kition as well as to all Late Bronze Age towns in Cyprus. Enkomi suffered the same fate and its inhabitants gradually abandoned it in order to build another town nearer to the sea, at Salamis.[72] At Kition the mudbrick superstructure of the city wall fell onto the street which runs parallel to the rectangular bastions and over the adjacent areas. Large portions of this wall, including complete mudbricks, were found during the excavation exactly as they fell on the street, sealing pottery of the second quarter of the eleventh century BC. It is obvious that afterwards neither the street nor the city wall were reconstructed at this site. The roof of the workshops and their walls collapsed, breaking the enormous pithoi on their floors. The large ashlar block foundations of the propylaeum of Temenos B broke in two, and parts of the ashlar block walls of the building in Area I were dislocated. The catastrophe was so considerable that the buildings must have been abandoned for a few years. During this period an alluvial deposit of sand was formed above floor II of the open courtyard of Temenos A, at least on those parts which were not covered by the debris from the fallen walls of adjoining buildings.

After this catastrophe and the subsequent abandonment of other Late Bronze Age towns of Cyprus, like Enkomi, probably as a result of the silting up of their inner harbours, Kition was rebuilt on a major scale. New houses were built in Area I, often following a different orientation from the houses of the previous period, but in some cases the foundations of the older houses were re-used. Thick hard floors belonging to this period, floor I, have been found throughout Areas I and II, which shows that the town must have been entirely rebuilt with the exception of its walls. The two temples and the two temene retained their plan as did the workshops. In Temenos A, however, the rectangular built altar with the horns of consecration was abandoned, probably owing to the considerable rising of the floor, and a new one was made of rectangular stone blocks measuring 1·20 m × 1·05 m, about 20 cm above floor level and directly against the north wall of the temple. Distinct traces of fire on its concave surface justify this identification. The north boundaries of the temenos were now marked by a wall of mudbricks, 1 m thick, which followed the line of the fallen city wall but about 2 m inward. Thus the width of the new temenos was reduced to 8 m. Floor I, built above the debris of the fallen roofs and walls of the previous period, is quite high, in several cases almost 50 cm above bedrock.

Plate 64

These new structures seem to have been used for a very short time. The pottery which has been found on floor I, White Painted I ware (with no Bichrome I) of the earliest type, is not later than *c.* 1000 BC. In a shallow pit in the area of old Room 16 a deposit (*bothros*) of votive offerings was found, put away by those who, as we shall see below, re-used the temple in the ninth century BC. These include terracotta figurines of a goddess with lifted arms and a high *polos* above the forehead, a type which corresponds with the sub-Minoan fertility goddess of Crete. There are also three fragmentary clay models of sanctuaries (*naiskoi*) of a type which also originated in sub-Minoan Crete. This offers further evidence in favour of the suggestion that Cretan elements were included among the refugees who settled in Cyprus after the Dorian invasion. There are also miniature votive dishes which, together with the naiskoi and the terracottas, appear to have been offered to the temple. Similar terracotta figurines were also found at Enkomi in the sanctuary of the Ingot God which was used for a while even after the earthquake had

Plate 65

Plates 66, 67

destroyed the town. This is further proof of the uniformity of religious beliefs at both Enkomi and Kition.

Fig. 15

In Temple 4 various phases of floor I have been discovered: floor Ia lay 25–30 cm above floor II, and showed two major phases of occupation. The earlier phase was represented by a well-constructed chavara floor which produced quantities of bone and charcoal and White Painted I sherds. A second chavara floor, 10 cm above the former, was covered with mudbrick debris and small stones and represents the later phase.

Floor I was a greenish-coloured alluvial soil floor covered with charcoal. This charcoal represents the destruction of 1000 BC and it is covered by a deposit of alluvial soil and a further accumulation of sterile red soil, illustrating the subsequent abandonment of this area of Kition for about 150 years. Floor I also produced quantities of White Painted I pottery.

The wall plan of the temple of floors II and III was re-used for floors I and Ia. In the floor I period, however, the floor level had risen to cover the original bench slabs as seen along the northern wall, and only the vertical ashlar blocks of the original wall were re-used. No column bases were found either for floor I or Ia.

Plate 68

The altar for floors I and Ia (labelled Altar E) was constructed on floor Ia and re-used, with an enlargement of the hearth pit, on floor I. It is a structure of mudbrick, chavara and limestone and lies on the central north–south axis of the courtyard and slightly to the north of its central east–west axis. It consists of a deep (23 cm) hearth pit (diameter 1·20 m) to the west, enclosed within a three-quarter circle wall of chavara and mudbrick, and a table of offerings, if it may so be called, immediately to the east. The chavara and mudbrick wall and the hearth it encloses belong only to floor I. A section left through the centre of the floor I hearth pit shows that the hearth of floor Ia was considerably smaller (diameter 35 cm) and there is evidence that it was also enclosed by a low chavara wall.

The table of offerings is in the form of an irregular rectangle, narrowing towards the east. Its construction consists of a very large drafted ashlar block 'fenced in' on its four sides by a double row of vertical well-dressed limestone slabs. Almost all of these slabs measure

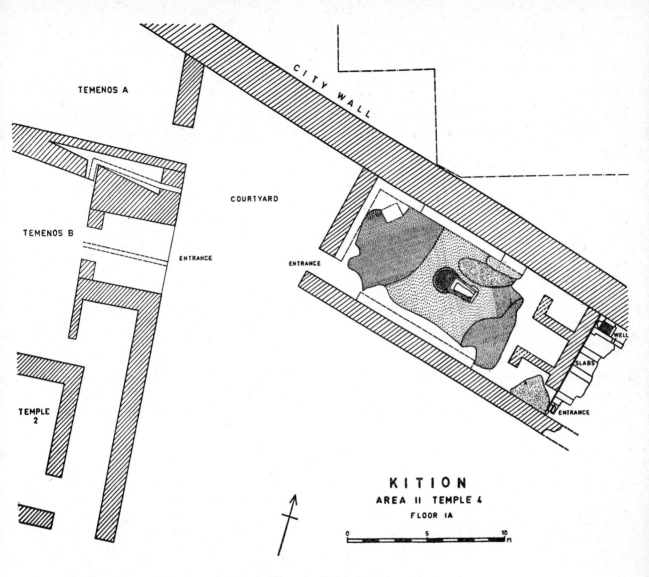

15   Plan of the modifications in architectural features of Temple 4 (floor Ia)

53 cm in width and 9 cm in thickness – this suggests that before being re-used for the altar they all came from the same original construction. The large drafted block was found resting neatly on the easternmost of the three east–west line column bases on floors II and III, using it as a foundation stone. Two limestone slabs were found lying horizontally over the drafted block, probably placed there to provide a level table surface. The overall length of Altar E (east–west) is 2·95 m. It is orientated toward the holy-of-holies to the east.

93

There are no signs of any metallurgical activity during this short revival of Kition after 1050 BC. The workshops must have been used for other purposes, probably as storerooms of the temple. In the meantime the inner harbour and the navigable channel which connected it with the sea may have silted up and been damaged owing to the earthquake. This may have been the main cause for the abandonment of this part of Kition (Area II) from the late eleventh to the late ninth century BC, and the shifting of the town to another site, probably nearer to the sea. That the buildings were abandoned is proved by the fact that thick layers of alluvial sand were deposited on floor I of the various rooms and on the floors of the two temene, well before the collapse of the walls.

Future investigations in other parts of Kition will one day reveal the remains of this new town. In the meantime its cemetery has been discovered, lying about 400 m west of Area I, in the Chrysosotiros quarter of modern Larnaca. Tombs of the Cypro–Geometric I and II periods (tenth and ninth centuries BC) have been found in this area and contain rich ceramic material.

V The Phoenicians at Kition

The initial stage of the Phoenician penetration to the West is still not fixed with certainty, though the general tendency is to place it c. 800 BC.[73] We shall not discuss this problem as a whole, but the suggestion is here put forward that there may have been Phoenicians in Cyprus at least about one hundred years earlier than the accepted date. A funerary inscription from Cyprus – unfortunately of no precise provenance – written in Phoenician, is dated shortly after 900 BC. The earliest Phoenician pottery found in Cyprus – the so-called 'Red Slip' ware – is now dated to the ninth century BC. This should not be surprising. During the first half of the eleventh century BC Syro–Palestinian influences were already evident on the island. There are several shapes of Proto-White Painted ware which are imitations of Syro–Palestinian vases and actual Syro–Palestinian pilgrim flasks are quite common in tombs.[74] Out of five tombs of the first half of the eleventh century which we excavated recently northeast of Salamis three contained a Syro–Palestinian pilgrim flask. There may have been a modest influx of Phoenicians already in the eleventh century, existing alongside the Aegean colonists who came to the island in successive waves. The myth of the foundation of Kition by King Belos, king of the Sidonians, who helped the Achaean Teukros to take possession of Salamis, may reflect the situation which we described above.[75]

There is literary evidence that the king of Tyre, Hiram I, at the start of his reign had to suppress a revolt of the people of Kiti(on) on the island of Cyprus.[76] If this information is correct then we have to accept that Kition was already under Tyrian rule at the beginning of the tenth century BC during the reign of Hiram's father Abibaal. Menander states that Hiram undertook a campaign against the Itykaians who had not paid their tribute and when he had again made them subject to him, he returned home. Several scholars have proposed Κιταῖος for Ἰτυκαῖος, meaning the inhabitants of Kition. Another argument in favour of Kition and not Utica in North Africa, is the fact that Hiram undertook this expedition at the beginning of his reign and a long journey to Utica would have been inconceivable and dangerous. It is after the Phoenicians established a stronghold at Kition that they ventured to expand westwards under King Ethbaal to the coast of North Africa.

The earliest documents which mention the presence of Phoenicians in Cyprus are the inscriptions on bronze bowls which are said to have been found near Amathus and which were dedicated by the governor of Khardihadast to Baal of Lebanon.[77] The governor is referred to as 'servant of Hiram, king of the Sidonians'. The king is Hiram II of Tyre, who reigned during the later part of the eighth century. Khardihadast, the 'New City', is accepted as being Kition[78] and thus we may take the above as evidence that by the end of the eighth century BC Kition was a Tyrian colony. The Late Bronze Age town which was abandoned *c.* 1000 BC may have been remembered by those who named its successor Khardihadast or 'New City'.

Cyprus, as noted earlier, was known as a naval power in the Bible and it provided wood for the construction of ships for Tyre. If Cyprus provided wood for the Phoenician ships it is not surprising that the Phoenicians sought to build a stronghold on the island so early. We know that they must have also exploited the island's rich copper mines.

Stratigraphic observations in Area II have shown that between 1000 BC and the end of the ninth century there was a hiatus which we have interpreted as a result of the abandonment of this part of the town. At the end of the ninth century BC, however, there must have been a revival on a large scale. Fine Samaria ware shallow bowls and Red Slip I ware jugs are found abundantly above the layer of alluvium which represents the abandonment. They rest on a floor which is associated with buildings which will be described below.

Temple 1. Careful stratigraphic observations outside the north wall of the courtyard of Temple 1 in Temenos A showed a continuous succession of floors from the thirteenth century to *c.* 1000

BC, and above these, a floor which abuts directly against the outer façade of the north wall, thereby indicating that it was standing and probably in use at the end of the ninth century BC. Inside the temple courtyard, however, the ninth-century floor was found directly on the bedrock, without any earlier floors below it, though several Late Bronze Age sherds were found between this floor and the bedrock in hollow cavities on the rock. It has now been established that sometime after the middle of the ninth century BC the foundations of the Late Bronze Age Temple 1 were re-used for another temple. The solid thick walls of the courtyard of Temple 1 must have been outstanding among the ruins of the abandoned sacred quarter, so that the newcomers used the already existing foundations in order to build their own edifice, again a temple. They respectfully collected the few offerings which they found inside the old temple, a few terracotta figurines of the goddess with lifted arms, fragmentary naiskoi and votive miniature dishes mentioned earlier, and placed them in a shallow pit, a bothros (labelled bothros 1), outside the north wall of the temple in the old Temenos A. The new temple, as already mentioned, was built on the foundations of old Temple 1, but now the south wall of the latter was abolished, its ashlar blocks of hard limestone were removed and only the foundations of large stones remained, unseen since they were concealed by the floor of the new temple courtyard. The south wall of the earlier corridor now became the south wall of the courtyard, thereby enlarging it considerably by taking into it the width of the old corridor. In the northern wall the opening which communicated with workshop Room 12 was blocked up.

Fig. 18

The holy-of-holies on the western part of old Temple 1 now became a long and narrow corridor occupying the whole width of the western side of the courtyard (22 m). Its inner width is 2·50 m. It had three entrances from the courtyard, a central one and two lateral. Probably the images of the divinity and two companions were kept in the holy-of-holies, the Phoenician *debir*, and could be seen through each of the three doors. Material used to build the holy-of-holies was taken from amongst the large stones of the nearby Late Bronze Age city wall. Only their upper part was dressed with inset ashlar blocks,

Plate 69

evidently because they were not seen if the floor was raised about 1 m higher than the floor level of the courtyard. One could reach the holy-of-holies through staircases in each door, but no traces of them have survived. On either side of the central entrance, outside the holy-of-holies, there were two pillars built of small ashlar blocks on all four sides and filled with rubble in the middle; they measure 2·20 m × 1·50 m at their base and one of them is preserved to a height of 1 m. The second one was destroyed by stone robbers and only a part of it survives. These two rectangular pillars, which may have been thinner at the top, were probably free-standing, since the roof of the porticos in the courtyard, as we shall see below, was supported on wooden columns. This arrangement recalls the tri-partite façade of the temple of Aphrodite at Paphos as it is represen-ted on Roman coins, at the top of which there may have been horns of consecration or a capital.[79] Such pillars are also known from the Bible, namely the two bronze pillars Jachin and Boaz of the Solo-monic temple in Jerusalem,[80] though their exact position in the architectural plan of the temple is unrecorded. Similar pillars have been found on either side of the entrance to the holy-of-holies of the recently discovered temple at Arad, and they are also known from the representation of the temple of Melkarth at Tyre.[81] Near these two pillars, slightly above floor level, there was a table of offerings consisting of one large rectangular slab of local gypsum, measuring 2·16 m × 86 cm with three perforations through it.

The large rectangular courtyard of the temple was partly roofed; along its south and north sides were two porticos whose roof was supported on a double row of pillars, leaving a space in the middle open to the sky, 4·40 m wide. The width of each portico was about 7 m. There were seven pillars in each row, thus making a total of twenty-eight. They had rectangular bases of hard limestone, measur-ing 90 cm × 75 cm. Of these six still survive *in situ*, the others were re-used as building material in subsequent periods, but traces of their position in the bedrock are distinct. They have a rectangular socket in the middle to receive a wooden pillar. All round the socket the surface of the stone is slightly worn and of a lighter colour, forming a neat rectangle which measures 60 cm × 40 cm, indicating that the

Plate 70

Plate 71

Plate 72

wooden pillars were rectangular and that they were 60 cm × 40 cm thick. In order to place these twenty-eight pillar bases, which occupy a considerable space of the courtyard, the builders found it necessary to remove all the soil of the courtyard of the old temple (i.e. all the floors) down to bedrock, in order to trace and dig the pits for the bases which are symmetrically placed. By doing this, however, they removed all the stratigraphic evidence for old Temple 1, as mentioned earlier.

There were two entrances to the courtyard of the temple. The propylaeum entrance to the courtyard of the old temple, at the north-eastern corner of the courtyard, was retained. The second entrance at the south-eastern corner was enlarged and access to it was made possible through a ramp paved with large pebbles and bordered by ashlar blocks. The entrance at the south-western corner was abolished and gave way to the holy-of-holies. The large rough stones at the outside of the courtyard were carefully removed and were replaced by large ashlar blocks, probably taken from old Temple 2 and also from the abolished south wall of the old court-yard. These ashlar blocks, often larger and higher than those of the inside surface of the walls, are of the same quality as the Late Bronze Age ashlar blocks and show exactly the same quality of carving. Some of them are 3·50 m long and 1·50 m high. They are particularly monumental along the outside façade of the south wall. The east wall of the courtyard also had its façade rebuilt of ashlar blocks, with the exception of the north wall, at least not from the foundation level. The reason may be that the outside surface of this wall was covered to a considerable height by the debris of the Late Bronze Age workshops which were never restored by the new-comers. The thickness of the south wall of the courtyard is 1·50 m. On its outside surface there are several graffiti of roughly drawn ships characteristic of the sea-faring race of the Phoenicians. Though the ashlar blocks were taken from the Late Bronze Age temple, the re-building of the façades must have required more stone to be carried and others to be replaced. In fact this is clear along the inner façade of the north wall, some of the blocks of which were replaced and others were patched; probably they suffered from weathering during

Plate 73

Plate 74

the 150 years of abandonment. The stone bases of the wooden pillars, the two built pillars on either side of the central entrance to the holy-of-holies, all attest expert masons. Since we know that Kition was a Tyrian colony we may legitimately evoke the craftsmanship of the Tyrian builders, who also built the temple of Solomon in Jerusalem.[82] It can be assumed that the wooden pillars were of cedar imported from the Lebanon.

Temple 2 was not rebuilt. Of the north wall only a few rubble stones remain above bedrock; of the other walls only those of the lower course remained *in situ*. The whole area in front of the east façade of the new temple, which includes the site of old Temenos B and Temple 2, was covered up with the fallen mudbricks, the debris of the walls of the Late Bronze Age buildings. It was levelled up and a new courtyard was created on the same foundations as and following exactly the boundaries of Temenos B on the north and east sides and those of old Temple 2 on the south side. Thus a new temenos, measuring 23·60 m north–south (maximum) and 19·20 m east–west, was created in front of the new temple. The altar of the previous temenos, constructed at floor II, was retained after repair. The monumental propylaeum at the entrance was also retained; a well was sunk near the south-eastern corner of the temenos. Outside the open courtyard, symmetrically arranged on either side of the entrance, were two pits dug into the bedrock, 50 cm deep and 50 cm in diameter, which contained reddish soil and nothing else. These may have been pits for two sacred trees on either side of the entrance to the sacred area. Such trees appear on either side of the façade of a temple on an eighth-century BC Cypriote vase and may recall the two biblical trees of Paradise.[83]

Plate 75

In **Temenos A** a new altar, next to the one of the previous period, was built of rectangular ashlar blocks of soft sandstone. It is rectangular, measuring 1·30 m × 1.37 m and 50 cm high; it rests on the alluvial deposit of floor I of the preceding period. Thus a magnificent new sacred area was created exactly on the site of the earlier one and partly with material taken from the old temples. Was this a symbolic gesture on the part of the Phoenicians to demonstrate their domination over the New City?

From the material which was discovered on the floor of the courtyard of the temple one may suggest a terminal date for its construction. Large quantities of Samaria ware shallow bowls, with a fine
red glossy slip on their surface and incised circles on their base have
been found on the floor of the lowest (earliest) courtyard, floor 3,
and particularly near the table of offerings; they were mixed with
ashes and charcoal, which may indicate that this material should be
associated with the destruction, possibly by fire, of the first temple.
The quantities of charcoal may come from the beams of the burnt
roof of the porticos as well as the wooden pillars. The Samaria
ware and other fragments of Red Slip ware jugs date this destruction
to *c.* 800 BC. The date of the construction of the first temple must
also be ascertained. But since nothing has been found in the courtyard or outside it, in the deposits (bothroi), which we shall describe
below, that could date earlier than the middle of the ninth century
BC, it can be assumed that it was constructed round about the middle
of the ninth century BC. If we assume that the Phoenicians started
colonizing Kition at the beginning of the ninth century BC, as the
earliest Phoenician inscription found in Cyprus may imply, then it
is quite reasonable to assume that by the middle of that century they
were in full control of the city.

Bothroi. The offerings placed in the temple during the first
phase of its existence were placed, after each destruction, in shallow
pits (bothroi) in the courtyard of the temenos to the east of the temple
and within the holy-of-holies. Every time the temple was filled with
offerings till there was no space for more, they would be removed,
placed in such bothroi and covered up again. This may have been the
case with bothros 9, in the open courtyard in front of the temple.
The same procedure must have been followed after the destruction of
the temple, thereby creating bothroi 3 and 4 in the holy-of-holies
and bothros 12 in front of the holy-of-holies near the table of offerings.
Bothros 9 was the largest of the two and contained sherds in vast
quantities which gave the impression that they were smashed and
walked upon. These, when mended, made up dozens of complete
vases, particularly large storage jars but also fine pottery, both local
and Phoenician. The fine quality Samaria ware is especially worthy of

Plate 76

Plate 77

Plate 78

note. An extraordinary vase of this ware was reconstructed from fragments found near bothros 12. It is a double bowl of ritual character, such as have been found in other parts of the Phoenician world, but the Kition specimen is by far the finest and one of the largest, measuring 34 cm in diameter and 21 cm in height.

Plate 79

Masks. About a dozen oxen skulls were found on the earliest floor of the temple. They were grouped together, not very far from the table of offerings. When they were restored it became clear that the back part had been purposely cut and cleaned of all projecting

Plates 80, 81

bones so that the skulls could be worn as masks, probably by the priests, during ritual ceremonies. Votive masks in clay have been found at Kition, dating to the twelfth and eleventh centuries BC. An

Plate XVI

early eleventh-century mask was found on floor 1 of a building which may prove to be a sanctuary.

The wearing of skulls has a very long tradition in Cyprus.[84] Already in the Early Bronze Age skulls of bulls were placed on wooden poles and kept in the most sacred part of sanctuaries, as is clearly depicted on clay models of such sanctuaries. During the Late Bronze Age the same practice was observed at Enkomi, where in the temple of the 'Horned God' and the temple of the 'Ingot God' (dating to the

---

XIV Copper slag on floor III of Room 14 of the industrial complex

XV The three bronze objects of the foundation deposit from Temple 4: two unfinished agricultural tools (ploughshares?) and a large peg

XVI Clay votive mask found at the end of 1974 in a partly excavated public building (perhaps a temple?). Early eleventh century BC. A similar clay mask, also painted black and red, was found in the sanctuary of the Ingot God at Enkomi and dates to the same period

XVII–XVIII Miniature vases from the foundation deposit in the south-east corner of the temple of Astarte, after cleaning: Black Slip vases from bothros 10 (XVII); Black-on-Red juglets from bothros 10 (XVIII)

XIX Bronze statuette found outside the courtyard of the temple of Astarte, on a layer corresponding to floor 2a

XX Scarabs, pendants and amulets of faience found in bothroi corresponding to the third period of the temple of Astarte

XIV

XV

XVI

XVII

XVIII

XIX

XX

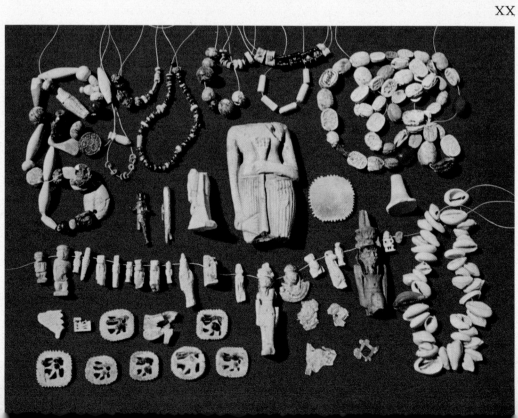

twelfth century BC), numerous skulls of oxen were found with their back parts cleaned in order to be worn as masks. In the temple of the 'Horned God' they were found near the altar with a large number of bowls and other offerings. It is significant that in both these temples the bronze cult statues represent the god wearing a helmet with horns. The purpose was to enter into direct association with the god by putting on his divine emblem and thereby acquire some of his qualities. The same idea existed both in the Aegean and the Near East, where Minotaurs and Bull-men dominated for centuries religious scenes as they appear in art. There is literary confirmation of this custom for a later period. The writer Lucian in his treatise *De Dea Syria* (*On the Syrian Goddess*) describes a practice, according to which 'when a man goes as a worshipper for the first time to Hierapolis [in Syria], he cuts his hair, then he sacrifices a lamb, he kneels down and puts the animal's head and feet on his own head, and prays to the gods to accept his sacrifice' (Lucian, *De Dea Syria*, 60).

Archaeological discoveries show that this custom was practised widely in Cyprus during the Archaic period (seventh and sixth centuries BC). Terracotta figurines found on the south coast at Kourion in the precinct of the temple of Apollo Hylates and in the sanctuary of Ayia Irini on the northern coast, represent priests wearing bull's masks.[85] The skulls themselves may have been sewn onto cloth or leather so as to create a real mask. On the masks of the figurines part of the dewlap is also represented. It is easy to imagine priests and worshippers wearing such masks and moving in procession through the open courtyard, sacrificing to the divinity, and then marching through the colonnaded porticos of the temple courtyard, where they placed gifts on the table of offerings, facing the sacred image of the deity which was visible through the central door of the holy-of-holies.

Plate 82

The sacrifice of lambs and sheep in general must have been a very frequent practice in the Phoenician temple of Kition. Large quantities of sheep bones were found in the bothroi outside the great temple and also outside Temple 4 (see below). Some of these bones were also found in a carbonized condition among the ashes of altars in the temenos of the Phoenician period.

Plate 83

As to the identity of the divinity which was worshipped in the temple there is valuable epigraphic evidence. In 1969 a fragmentary bowl of Phoenician Red Slip ware was found in the temple court-yard, corresponding stratigraphically to the first period of the temple, which has a long inscription engraved after firing on its outside surface. The inscription, in spite of its lacunae, is quite long; palaeo-graphically and independently of its stratigraphic associations, it was dated by experts to the end of the ninth century BC, which conforms perfectly with the date which we have given to the first temple. Professor A. Dupont-Sommer has deciphered this inscription and his decipherment throws ample light on the identity of the divinity worshipped in the temple as well as on the religious practices which were performed in it.[86] The translation as proposed by Professor Dupont-Sommer is as follows:

(1) In memorial. ML had his hair (herein) shaved and prayed to Lady Astarte and Astarte listened to his prayer (2) And were offered (as a sacrifice): on the part of ML, a sheep and a lamb, together (3) with this hair; on the part of the family of ML, a lamb. This vase (4) ML filled with his hair (herein) . . . seven in number, because of the prayer made in Tamassos (5) . . . the gift . . . which he liked . . . (6) Tamassos. . . .

It is clear from the above that ML, which may be identified with the well-known Phoenician name Moula, probably a citizen of Tamassos, went as a worshipper together with his family to the temple of Astarte. We shall see later on that there was a temple of Astarte at Kition which is known from another inscription. The ritual performances described on the bowl recall in a striking manner the ritual ceremonies which are described by Lucian about one thousand years later. As well as observing the worshippers at Hiera-polis, Lucian mentions that, just before their marriage, boys and girls go to the temple, have their hair cut and put it in vases of gold or silver which are fixed in the temple and inscribe their names thereon. Lucian adds that he did exactly the same when a young man, and that his own hair was in such a bowl, with his name en-graved on it, in the temple. An inscription, painted in black ink on both sides of a small marble plaque now in the British Museum, was discovered during the British levelling operations at the Acropolis of Kition, described in Chapter I. The inscription, published for the first time by Ernest Renan in 1881, is dated to the fourth century BC and refers to the accounts of the temple of Astarte, enumerating several categories of persons who were employed in the temple together with their renumeration.[87] Among them are the 'sacred barbers' whose function has now become clear since the discovery of the inscribed bowl.

This identification is further strengthened by historical circumstances. The years round the mid-ninth century BC coincide with the long and prosperous reign of Ethbaal, king of the Tyrians and the Sidonians, who reigned for thirty-two years (887–856 BC). Prior to becoming king he was a high priest of Astarte and when he ascended the throne he instituted her cult as the official cult of his kingdom. It is natural then, that in a major Phoenician colony like Kition, Temple I, which was dedicated to a female goddess attested by votive terracottas of the Astarte type, should have been rebuilt by King Ethbaal as a temple of Astarte, since Kition was part of his kingdom.[88]

The **Temple of Astarte** at Kition must have been an important one, equal perhaps to the famous temple of Aphrodite at Paphos (mentioned in inscriptions as Astarte Paphia). Recent excavations at Paphos have in fact revealed that it had exactly the same history as that of Kition: it was first built at the end of the thirteenth century BC (capitals of exactly the same style as those from Kition were found at the temple site in 1973), and continued in existence through the first millennium BC down to the Roman period. The representations of this temple on Roman coins from Paphos show the three entrances to the holy-of-holies, with free-standing pillars on either side of the central entrance exactly as at Kition. In front of the holy-of-holies is the courtyard.[89]

Plate 71

The personnel employed in the temple of Astarte of Kition is described in detail on the inscription in the British Museum and indicates both its importance and size. There were guards, numerous servants, bakers, barbers, scribes and sacred prostitutes. This precious document, being an administrative account of the personnel and their salaries for a certain period, offers a vivid picture of the life in the temple, and may be supplemented by what Herodotus tells us about the temple of Astarte at Paphos.[90]

We have suggested that the first temple of Astarte was destroyed by fire, and was soon rebuilt. In the south-west corner of the court-yard of the temple a large number of miniature bowls and juglets, mostly of Black-on-Red, Black Slip and Red Slip wares, were found, together with carbonized animal bones, all mixed with ashes. There was also an iron skewer and an iron knife. All these were covered by the subsequent floor of the temple, floor 2a, which means that they were deposited before the inauguration of the new (second) temple. The fact that most of them were found intact suggests that we do not have here an ordinary deposit (bothros) where vases are usually crushed, but a deposit associated with a ceremony. This may have been a foundation ceremony, with foundation deposits and a sacrifice, performed in one of the corners of the temple (not under a wall, since it was only the columns and the roof of the temple which were rebuilt, not the walls). This would assure the goddess that her new temple would not have the same fate as the first one.

Fig. 19

The second temple at floor 2a undergoes several modifications in the interior, but the general layout remains the same. The two lateral entrances to the holy-of-holies were abolished and only the central one was maintained. The major change in the courtyard consisted in the abandonment of the double colonnade for each portico and the construction of two rows of pillars, built of masonry, one row for each portico. There were six pillars in each row, and they are all preserved except two. They measure 1·40 m × 1·40 m and do not have a cavity in the centre, since the wooden pillars were abolished.

Plate 85

For the bases of these pillars some of the old bases were re-used, but in one case a large stone capital of the Late Bronze Age Temple 1 was used. The table of offerings near the holy-of-holies remained the same. In the open courtyard to the east of the temple, the old altar was abolished and a new one, rectangular in shape, with stone blocks on all four sides and an orthostat in the middle, was built near the north-western entrance to the temple courtyard. Those who pro-ceeded from the open courtyard to the temple courtyard had the new

Plate 86

altar on their left-hand side. The main entrance to the open courtyard, on the east, was embellished and turned into an imposing
propylaeum, measuring 5·40 m in length and 4·20 m in width. The
side walls are 1·40 m thick, and were constructed of rather small
blocks of soft sandstone which have now deteriorated. The northern
border wall of the open courtyard was robbed of its stones at a later
date. A small room was built against the north wall of the propylaeum
to the open courtyard, probably a storeroom. In the open courtyard
along the north wall of the temple (Temenos A) the altar which was
built against the wall was covered over by the new floor, and a new
built altar was created right on top of the old altar with the horns of
consecration of the Late Bronze Age temenos. Between the lower
part of this new altar and the top of the Late Bronze Age altar there is
a layer of soil about 15 cm thick, which excludes the possibility of
continuous use of the same altar.

The second period of the temple is the longest, and we have
assigned to it 200 years, from approximately 800–600 B C. This is one
of the richest periods in the history of the temple. Its early part corresponds to the reign of Hiram II who, as we know, paid tribute
to King Tiglatpileser III of Assyria (745–727 B C).[91] It is also known
that the king of Khardihadast (Kition) paid tribute to King Hiram II,
being his 'servant'. In 709 B C Cyprus was occupied by the Assyrians
and, according to an inscribed stele found at Kition and now in Berlin, the seven kings of Cyprus 'kissed his feet'. This signifies, no
doubt, that the special relations which existed between Kition and
the mother city Tyre were interrupted or that they were placed on
another basis. It is during this period that we may assign the campaign
of Eloulaios against Kition which revolted against Tyrian rule,
probably at the instigation of the Greek cities of the island who were
on good relations with Sargon II. The latter allowed a certain
degree of autonomy to the Cypriote kings provided they paid their
tribute regularly. Sennacherib of Assyria interpreted the action of
Eloulaios as a declaration of war. In 701 B C he occupied the Tyrian
kingdom except Tyre itself and Eloulaios fled to Kition where he
died in 694 B C. On the famous prism of Esarhaddon (680–669 B C)
ten kings of the land of 'Yatnana [Cyprus] in the middle of the sea'

are recorded, among whom is Damasu of Khardihadast (Kition).[92] This means that the governor of the town, who was 'servant of Hiram', was appointed as king by the Assyrians and that Kition could now follow a policy independent of Tyre. This, however, does not mean that the Phoenicians lost control of Kition in any way. On the contrary they may have collaborated more faithfully with the Assyrian masters of the island than the other kings whose names, as they appear on the Esarhaddon prism, appear to be Greek. They must have developed their commercial fleet and carried out trade with both East and West. It is not surprising that Cyprus appears in the list of thalassocracies mentioned by Eusebius.[93]

The wealth of the bothroi which correspond to this period is indicative of the flourishing trade of Kition. Among the large jars reconstructed from the sherds of bothros 9 there are several which are imports from Athens. There are also fragments of Late Greek Geometric pottery from the Cyclades. This shows that Phoenician trade with the Aegean was flourishing and that the Greeks from Euboea, who set off for their eastward colonial expansion in the eighth century BC and whose presence has already been noted at Salamis,[94] may have had some relations, most probably commercial, with the Phoenicians of Kition. On the floor of the second Phoenician temple several objects have been found, of which the following may be mentioned:

Plate 87

(1) The ivory hilt of a bronze sword, preserving some of the bronze rivets which fastened the hilt to the blade; these have silver-plated heads, a fact which brings this sword within the group of 'silver-studded' swords, one of which was found in a seventh-century tomb at Salamis. These swords are of special importance for students of Homeric problems.[95]

Plate 88

(2) A statuette of a kneeling woman, 7 cm high, made of faience and painted with green or blue and yellow. The seated figure wears a high cylindrical polos and holds on her lap a kid or a gazelle. She kneels on a plinth which has in front of it a lion's head in relief. At the back of the statuette there is an infant in relief. The statuette is perforated from the top of the kalathos to the lion's head to contain a liquid. Professor Leclant, who will publish this statuette in detail,

proposes that it contained 'eau de juvence' from the Nile. Several similar Egyptian-looking statuettes are known from the Mediterranean and were one of the goods favoured by Phoenician traders.

Outside the temple courtyard in the open space to the south, two small bronze statuettes have been found, corresponding stratigraphically to the second temple. They represent male figures wearing a kilt, one with a lifted arm, in the characteristic attitude of blessing.

Plates 89, XIX

The third period of the temple, at floor 2, dates roughly from 600–450 BC. This coincides with the political *floruit* of the Phoenicians who took advantage of the Persian domination over Cyprus. After the failure of the Ionian revolt (499 BC) in which the Cypriots participated, the Persian rulers used the Phoenicians in the administration of the various kingdoms of the island. Kition must have been particularly favoured in such a political atmosphere. The target of the alliance between the Persians and the Phoenicians were the pro-Greek cities of Cyprus such as Idalion, which was attacked and conquered in 470 BC and was subsequently annexed to Kition. The Phoenician rulers of Kition gradually extended their influence, both political and cultural, over other towns of Cyprus, for example Amathus, Golgoi, Tamassos and Lapithos.[96]

The third period is one of great prosperity for the temple, as seen from the wealth of offerings found in the bothroi corresponding to it. They consist of scarabs, vases of faience and other exotic goods, including objects of ivory. All this implies that among the worshippers to the temple there may have been foreigners or Phoenicians who brought these goods from the countries with which they traded. Ionia may be included among these countries, to judge from the relatively high percentage of Ionic pottery found in the bothroi. The major architectural change within the courtyard of the temple during the third period is connected with the increase in the quantities of offerings which were dedicated in the temple. Thus two wide benches were built, one against the south wall of the courtyard and the other against the north wall. They are 1·15 m wide and 30 cm high; the one along the south side is 20 m long. Directly against the south wall of the courtyard, built at regular intervals, there are eleven rectangular pedestals, the top of which is at the same level

Plates 90, XX

Fig. 16

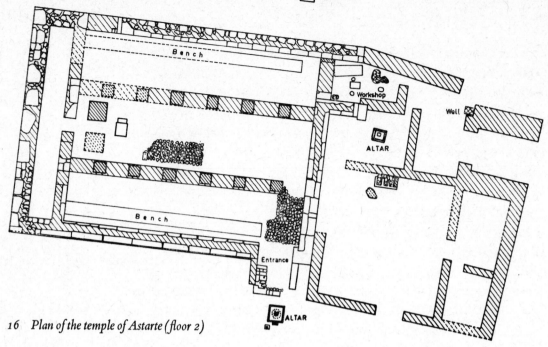

ALTAR B

Bench

Workshop

Well

ALTAR

ALTAR

Entrance

16   *Plan of the temple of Astarte (floor 2)*

with the top of the benches. These must have been also intended for
offerings, if not for statues. The benches are a common element in
Near Eastern sacred architecture, and examples have been found in
the recently excavated temple of Arad in Palestine.

Another major change in the courtyard is the building up with
masonry of the intercolumniations. It is quite unlikely, however, that
this masonry was higher than 50 cm from the level of floor 2 of the
courtyard. This masonry may have belonged to two other benches,
parallel to the ones along the north and south walls respectively, to
make room for the deposit of more offerings. It, however, is not
preserved to its original height and it is not easy to determine what
this might have been. If the masonry was as high as the pillars, then
the two porticos would have been in darkness. Those who
entered the temple courtyard through the south entrance (the floor
of which was now raised) could circulate in the south portico of the
courtyard and could also proceed to the central uncovered space of
the courtyard. It is not easy to say how they could proceed to the
north portico, but this may have been possible through a doorway
between two pillars, of which only the bases survive. The new floor

of the courtyard (floor 2) is now paved with pebbles and small flat stones; patches of this paving are still preserved. In front of the two rectangular pillars, on either side of the central entrance to the holy-of-holies, there is a large rectangular slab of local gypsum which is the new table of offerings, replacing a similar one which served the first and second temples. It measures 1·36 m × 1·20 m and has three perforations.

There is now only one entrance to the temple courtyard in its south-east corner; the second entrance in its north-east corner was blocked up with masonry, as we shall see below. In front of the south entrance, almost on the same axis, there is an altar, circular in shape, framed on all four sides with local gypsum slabs, forming a square 1·55 m × 1·55 m. The altar itself is of gypsum, with superimposed layers which bear distinct traces of fire at the top. It seems that the altar was repaired after a number of sacrifices. In the south-west corner of the temenos there was a rich bothros (no. 6), which produced, apart from pottery, chippings of ivory, indicating that there were ivory-carvers working near the temple who made relics for selling to the worshippers, who in their turn offered them to the temple. There were probably also other craftsmen in the vicinity, certainly smiths who produced small figurines, as we shall see below.

The same bothros also produced a fragment from a sixth-century BC local Cypriote bowl which bears the engraved name of Melkarth. A temple of Melkarth existed on the Acropolis of Kition from the seventh century BC onwards, and has been excavated by the Swedish Cyprus Expedition.[97] There were also terracotta statuettes, of which those representing pregnant women are particularly worthy of note. No doubt these were offerings of special significance to Astarte.

In the meantime significant changes took place within the temenos. The north-east entrance to the temple courtyard was abolished and blocked up with masonry. Its imposing propylaeum was squared off on the east side by walls built of rubble and thus a roughly rectangular room was created, measuring 6·50 m × 4 m with an entrance to the east. This room was used as a workshop for the smelting of copper. Quantities of copper slag were found on the floor of the workshop, together with ashes; small furnaces were also

Plate 91

Plate 92

found on the floor, which caused the darkening by fire of the façade of the ashlar blocks which formed the propylaeum of the previous periods. The altar which was built during the previous period next to the propylaeum was now enclosed within a rectangular room, the walls of which were of rubble, and which could communicate both with the rest of the open courtyard and with the workshop. Though the monumental propylaeum of the earlier period on the east wall of the temenos was retained, yet the division of the temenos into smaller compartments (there were two rectangular ones, communicating with one another, along the east side of the temenos) made the entrance rather inconvenient, and a new one was created on the south side of the temenos. This entrance gave access to the main part of the temenos which was now reduced to a rectangular courtyard, measuring 13 m × 12·70 m. The two rectangular rooms along the east side were probably storerooms. The idea of a workshop within the sacred area, communicating directly with the altar room of the temenos, recalls the Late Bronze Age arrangement. It is not easy to say whether this practice continued uninterruptedly from the Late Bronze Age onwards, and that these later workshops are still to be discovered elsewhere in the vicinity of the temple, or whether this is a revival with the symbolic presence of a small workshop; or even whether this small workshop had no significance other than to produce bronze statuettes for the temple.

A rectangular well, with walls built of stone, is to be found opposite the entrance to the workshop, against the north wall of the propylaeum. This may have been used for lustral purposes.

Plate 93

Three consecutive 'hearths' with thick traces of ashes inside them were found against the north wall of the new reduced temenos; they were probably meant for sacrifices. Animal bones have been found near the hearths.

The fourth and last period of the temple at floor 1 may be roughly dated from 450–312 BC. This was a crucial period for the Greek population of the island under the oppressive rule of the Persians, but quite a favourable one for the Phoenicians. Their political power increased, their collaboration with the Persians in the island's administration expanded and we know from Isokrates that a Phoenician king, Abdemon, was appointed at Salamis, 'the most Greek' of all the towns of Cyprus.[98] The efforts of the Cypriots to gain their freedom were often supported by the Athenians, who sent their general Kimon to free the island in 450 BC, but he died while besieging Kition in 449 BC. After this the Athenians signed what is known as the 'Peace of Kallias' with the Persians, by which Cyprus became part of the Persian fifth satrapy. The establishment of peaceful relations between Athens and Persians favoured Athenian trade with the Eastern Mediterranean. This is the period when Attic pottery is found in large quantities in Cyprus. Kition, too, must have been open to Athenian trade and the wealthy Kitians acquired some fine Attic Red-Figured vases, which they dedicated to the temple. The taste for the artistically superior products of Greek art, including terracotta figures, increased among the population of Kition and the contents of the bothroi of the last temple attest this. Political unrest, however, revived during the early part of the fourth century BC. The Athenians sent a fleet to Cyprus and Kition was captured in 388 BC. Its king, Melekiathon, was dethroned and an Athenian citizen called Demonikos was installed on the throne of Kition. Another treaty, however, known as the 'Peace of Antalkidas', was signed between Athens and Persia in 386 BC, by which Cyprus and the Greek cities of Asia were conceded to Persia. The new king of Kition, Pumiathon, strengthened his position, and extended his rule over Idalion and Tamassos. His superb gold coins, showing Heracles–Melkarth on the obverse and a lion attacking a stag on the reverse with legends in Phoenician, are indicative of his wealth and power.

Plates 94, 95

The Phoenicians had strong control over the town and the relations with Tyre, the 'metropolis' of Kition, were closer than ever. We know from an inscription on a sarcophagus that a 'minister or ambassador of Tyre' whose name was Eshmounadon was accredited in the court of Kition in the fourth century.[99] But at the same time the Kitians developed commercial relations with Athens. Large quantities of Attic Black-Glazed ware pottery have been found in the bothroi of the temples of Kition, as already mentioned above, and also some exquisite fragments from large Attic Red-Figured vessels. The Kitian merchants had an organized community in Piraeus and

Plates 96, 97

Plates 98, 99, 101
Plate 100

in 333/332 BC they applied for permission to build a temple of Aphrodite there.[100] In their own temples at Kition they placed terracotta statuettes of Attic provenance; their stone and marble sculpture often betrays influences from Greek sculpture. The well-known marble statue of Artemis from Kition, now in Vienna, is no doubt a work of art by a great Greek sculptor. A recently discovered marble base of a statue (found at the village of Kiti, near Larnaca) bears a long Phoenician inscription, mentioning a dedication of a statue to Eshmun by a certain BD for his son KLKY.[101] The inscription is dated to the forty-second year of King Pumiathon (320/319 BC) and he is referred to as king of Kition and Idalion – he had already lost Tamassos in about the thirtieth year of his reign. This is the latest inscription so far which refers to King Pumiathon.

The situation changed when Alexander the Great appeared on the political scene in the Eastern Mediterranean. Pumiathon was quick to foresee the political consequences and tried to win the favour of Alexander by presenting him with a sword, remarkable for its temper and light weight, as Plutarch records. But in spite of this he never won the confidence of Alexander. During the period of antagonism between the successors of Alexander, Pumiathon seems to have sided with Antigonus. Ptolemy I of Egypt put Pumiathon to death, burnt down the temple of Heracles–Melkarth, and thus the Phoenician dynasty of Kition was eclipsed. The temple of Astarte must have suffered the same fate.

Fig. 17

The architecture of the fourth period of the temple of Astarte is the least well preserved. This is unfortunate, because it could have given us useful information about the history and the general situation at Kition in a period during which the town was so much involved in the political fights between Greeks and Persians. There are sufficient elements to show that during this fourth period the central part of the temple courtyard was divided into six compartments, with an altar opposite the south entrance. These may have been compartments for storing objects. The actual architectural plan of the temple, however, is difficult to determine. The floor of the fourth temple has not been found, only the foundations of the walls of the compartments of the central part of what used to be the courtyard have

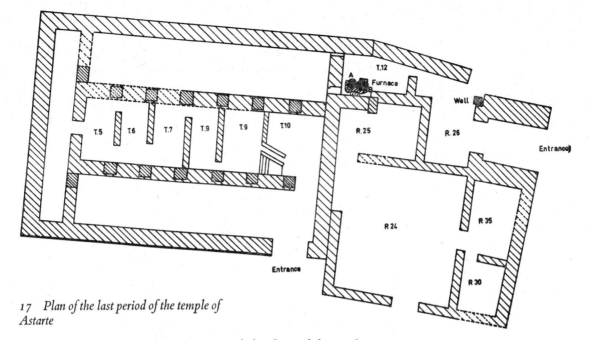

17　*Plan of the last period of the temple of*
Astarte

survived. The stone robbers removed the floor slabs; only one or two
still remain, showing that the floor was 1·50 m above the level
of the surface of the bedrock, i.e. 1·50 m above floor 3 of the first
Phoenician temple. Traces of altars built of ashlar blocks were found
in what used to be Temenos A, near the altars of the Late Bronze Age
and the earlier Phoenician period. But the general layout of the
temple is lost. We do not know whether the original orientation or
layout were kept or whether there were any modifications. All the
stones above the lower course of ashlar blocks of the original temple
have been removed.

　Temple 4 has more or less the same development as Temple 1.
After an abandonment of about 150 years, from *c.* 1000 BC to the
middle of the ninth century, a new Phoenician temple was built above
floor I, more or less on the foundations of the previous Late Bronze
Age temple. The earliest Phoenician temple is represented by floors
3 and 3a, corresponding to floor 3 of the great temple of Astarte.
This new temple has important changes in plan. The two small rectangular rooms of the holy-of-holies of floors I, II and III were
abandoned and instead a new sanctuary area was created by building
a wall in the same area, parallel to the eastern wall of the temple. The
space between this wall and the outer wall now formed a new

Fig. 18

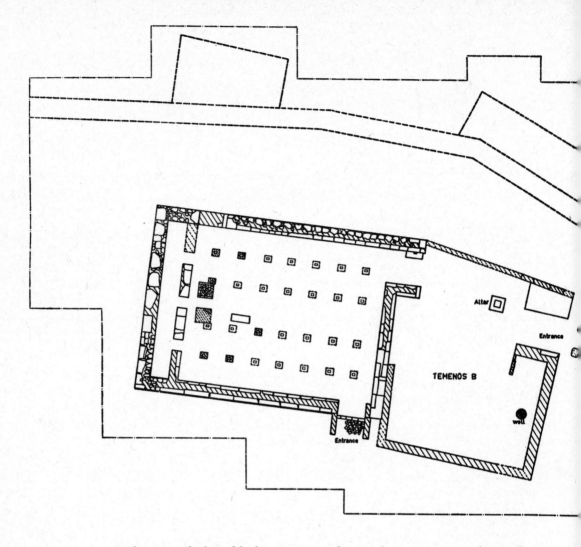

single room holy-of-holies, rectangular in shape, on a north-south axis and with a lateral entrance to the south to connect it with the courtyard. Only several blocks to the north survive of this new sanctuary wall. A looters' trench, which was dug to remove the other stones, follows the wall line. It contained Hellenistic sherds, indicating that the destruction and looting took place after the abandonment of the sacred area (after 312 BC). This new holy-of-holies measures 3·50 cm (east–west) by 5·30 cm (north–south).

The original eastern entrance to the temple was closed but the opening in the west wall was re-used and became the only entrance to the temple. The south and west walls of the temple of floors 3

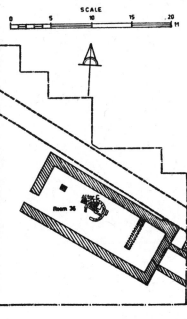

18 Plan of the great Phoenician temple of Astarte and Temple 4 (floor 3, Phoenician period)

and 3a and later periods follow the same line as the Late Bronze Age walls. The north wall, however, was built 60 cm inside the old wall and the east wall on the line of the outside face of the original. These walls, which are preserved only in the north-east corner, are of rubble construction. The courtyard in this period, excluding the thickness of the walls which we can no longer determine, measures 12 m (east–west) by 5·50 m (north–south).

Floor 3a was constructed of thick white gypsum with patches of red and green clay and some indications of ashes. It produced Red Slip ware pottery and is evidently an early phase of floor 3. The hard limestone bases for two columns on floor 3a were found lying

119

on a north–south line in front of the holy-of-holies. An iron knife was found between floors 3a and I.

The hearth of the altar (Altar D) for floor 3a lies directly above the hearth pit of Altar E and is of similar construction. This pit lies to the west of the table and is surrounded by a low, horseshoe-shaped enclosure wall. The wall, like that of Altar E, has a core of mudbrick and is covered with chavara and slopes outward. The hearth itself is rectangular in shape and contained ashes and a few bones and White Painted III ware sherds. The people who used floor 3a re-used the Altar E table as their own table of offerings. The two slabs of limestone placed horizontally over the big drafted block of Altar E may indicate an attempt by the floor 3a people to raise the level of the table surface. These two slabs were obviously part of the original Altar E as they are of the same width and thickness as the other slabs used in its construction; but it is impossible to ascertain whether they originally lay horizontally over the big block or were re-used in that position for Altar D. The western face of these slabs had been lined with plaster to protect them from the heat of the hearth fire.

Plate 102

The altar for floor 3 (Altar C) which overlies Altar D is also of similar construction but differs significantly in plan. Both the hearth to the west and the table to the east and an open space in front of them to the south are enclosed within the chavara and mudbrick wall. This wall has an entance 90 cm wide to the south-west where floor 3 is preserved. The total area inside the wall measures 2 m (east–west) by 1·85 m (north–south). The southern half of the enclosed area has been hollowed out to a depth of 10 cm below floor 3 to form a kind of sacred courtyard before the hearth and table. The hearth was roughly circular in shape and contained many successive layers of ashes to a depth of 14 cm. Of the table only the foundation stones remain and even they have been considerably disturbed. The two horizontal limestone slabs belonging to the surface of the Altars' E and D table were re-used as foundation stones. The upper stones of the table were probably removed during the construction of Altar B on floors 2 and 2a as this altar lies immediately over its south-east edge.

41 Detail of a wall in Area I, constructed of rubble in the lower part and in the upper of ashlar blocks. This new style of construction coincides with the arrival of the first Achaean colonists in Cyprus

42 One of the bastions in Area II (centre) built against the Cyclopean city wall (right), with a street running parallel to it (left)

43 General view of the city wall from the east, with Temenos A on the left between the city wall and the north wall of Temple I

44 Rectangular pool with pebbles in the bottom in the central part of the courtyard of Temple I. The pool is carved in the bedrock and during the Phoenician period it was filled with debris and was partly occupied by a stone pillar base

45 Detail of an ashlar block on the inner east façade of the courtyard of Temple I with engraved signs of the Cypro-Minoan syllabary along its upper edge

46 Detail of the inner face of the south wall of Temple 2 with ashlar blocks on rubble foundations. The rubble wall above the ashlar blocks is of a later period

47 The holy-of-holies of Temple 2 from the north. The façade of the parapet wall (facing the courtyard) is constructed of ashlar blocks. The thin wall dividing the holy-of-holies in two is of the following period

48 Rectangular altar at the western part of Temenos A (floor III) with a limestone block at its base shaped as horns of consecration, the symbol of the Creto-Mycenaean religion. Next to it (left), at a lower level, is the hearth-altar of Temple 3 of the previous period

49 Temenos B: a rectangular courtyard limited by the east wall of Temple 1 and the north wall of Temple 2. In the foreground (right) is its monumental propylaeum. Along the south side of the temenos are two stone capitals erected on rectangular pillars (modern reconstruction)

50 General view of Temenos
A from the east. In front of it
lies a triangular courtyard. In
the foreground is the western
part of Temple 4

51 Horns of consecration (two
blocks of hard limestone joined
together) from Temenos B

52 Reconstructed altar of the Myrtou sanctuary with horns of consecration at the top

53 Room 12 of the industrial complex with a bench against the west wall and a pit with stone anchor next to it

54   The industrial quarter at floor III from the west. In the foreground are two superimposed furnaces for the roasting of bones and the production of bone ash which was kept in pits and used as fluxing material for smelting

55 Bronze statue of the 'Ingot God' from Enkomi, standing on a base in the form of an oxhide ingot. Twelfth century BC

56 Bronze statuette in the Ashmolean Museum, Oxford, representing a nude 'Astarte' figure, standing on a base in the form of an oxhide ingot. Twelfth century BC

57 General view of Temple 4, floor III

58 Ivory handle found on floor III of the holy-of-holies of Temple 4. Its upper part is perforated twice on the sides and has a dowel hole through the cylindrical shaft, probably for a rod of ivory or other non-metallic material, since no traces of any corrosion were found on the sides of the dowel hole

59 Foundation deposits of bronze lying horizontally on mudbrick debris in the north-west corner of Temple 4

◀ 60 A paved area and a built well east of Temple 4 from the north. The paved floor abuts against the ashlar blocks of the outer façade of the east wall of the temple, of which only the flat foundation of stone anchors survives

◀ 61 Sling shot of unbaked clay found on floor II of Room 12 in the industrial quarter

◀ 62 The monumental propylaeum of Temenos B, in the foreground, for floor II

63 Proto-White Painted ware amphoriskos, associated with floor II. Early eleventh century BC

64 Temenos A from the west. To the right is a rectangular stone altar which replaced the altar with horns of consecration (left) of floor I. At a lower level are the foundations of Temple 3 and its hearth-altar

65 Terracotta figurine of a
female goddess with raised
arms found in a deposit outside
Temple 1 and belonging to the
last period of the temple
(floor I)

66, 67 Two clay models of
sanctuaries (naiskoi) found in a
deposit outside Temple 1 and
corresponding chronologically
to the last period of the temple
(floor I)

68 Altar E at floors Ia-I in the courtyard of Temple 4

69 The *debir* (holy-of-holies) of the great Phoenician temple from the south. On either side of its central entrance were two rectangular pillars (one has been destroyed) with a table of offerings in front of them

70 One of the two rectangular pillars on either side of the central entrance to the holy-of-holies of the great Phoenician temple

71 Roman coin illustrating the façade of the holy-of-holies of the temple of Astarte (Aphrodite) at Paphos. In front is the courtyard. The central entrance to the holy-of-holies and the two lateral entrances are clearly visible. On either side of the central entrance are two free-standing pillars

72 A rectangular pillar base of hard limestone found *in situ* on floor 3 of the courtyard of the great Phoenician temple. Round the rectangular socket the traces left by the wooden pillar are visible

73 Detail of the façade of the south wall of the courtyard of the great Phoenician temple showing graffiti of ships

74 The façade of the south wall of the courtyard
of the great Phoenician temple, from the south-west

There were three column bases on floor 3 in an east–west line along the northern side of the courtyard. The easternmost two flank each side of Altar C. The positions of these bases indicate that only the northern side of the courtyard was roofed, leaving the altar open to the sky.

Floor 3 itself consisted of grey clay with occasional spots of ferrous clay and chavara. Only a few sherds of Plain White ware, Black-on-Red and Samaria ware were found. Both floors 3 and 3a sloped down to the north.

Floors 2 and 2a, corresponding to floors 2 and 2a of the great temple of Astarte, were constructed of gypsum and both were overlaid by thick layers of occupation debris. These two floors, with a total thickness of 15–20 cm, represent an uninterrupted use of the temple for a period of several centuries. They produced shell, bone, charcoal, patches of ash, fragments of copper slag, and sherds of Plain White ware and Samaria ware.

From the evidence of the only remaining section of the floor 2 and 2a walls in the temple's north-west corner, it seems that the walls were rebuilt for floor 2a and again for floor 2. They follow substantially the same lines as the previous walls of floors 3 and 3a. The rectangular holy-of-holies remained in use as did the entrance in the west wall of the courtyard.

Fig. 19

Two circular altars were erected originally on floor 2a and were re-used on floor 2 near the centre of the temple courtyard. Altar B had a diameter of 1·40 m and a depth of 23 cm, and it was composed of a mudbrick and clay foundation on floor 2a, overlaid by several layers of chavara and ashes representing various rebuildings of the surface during use. In the floor 2 period the altar was topped with plaster and a circular pit (35 cm in diameter) was cut into the apex of the altar surface. This pit contained ashes to a depth of 7 cm.

Plate 103

Altar A, 90 cm to the east of Altar B, measured 1·70 m (north–south) by 1·55 m (east–west) by 26 cm deep. It was composed of layers of gypsum and chavara mixed with ashes. Two shallow bowls of Plain White ware were found *in situ* placed upside down on the outer rim of the altar. Similarly constructed altars are known from the sanctuaries of the Palace of Vouni near the north coast of Cyprus,

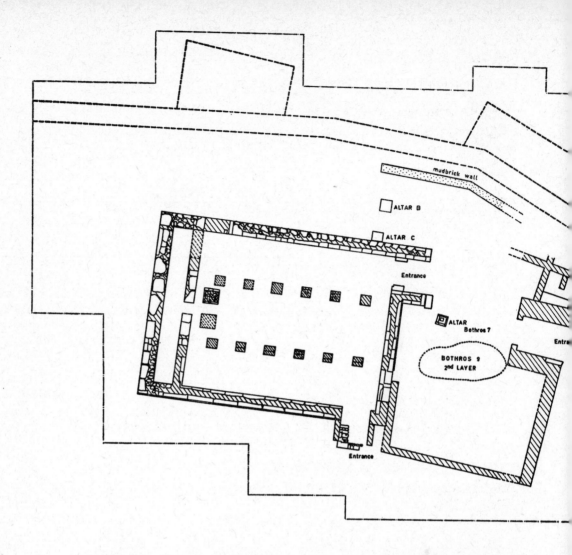

dating to the Classical period, and also from Kition itself: the altar of floor 2, in front of the south entrance to the temple of Astarte, is of the same construction.

A table of offerings, rising 25 cm above floor 2, was found in the south-east corner of the courtyard. The surface of this table is formed by two rectangular slabs of local marmara with smaller irregular stones abutting them on the east to form a rough square (1 m × 1 m approximately). This surface rests on a foundation of smaller rocks and broken pieces of marmara. The whole construction rests on floor 2a and must belong only to floor 2. A large patch of alluvial soil to the north of the table indicates that it was unroofed and exposed to the elements. Floor 2 probably represents the last period

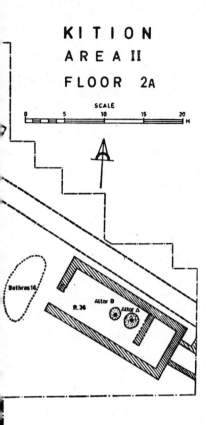

KITION
AREA II
FLOOR 2A

SCALE
0   5   10   15   20
M

Bothros 16

R.36   Altar B
       Altar A

19 Plan of the great Phoenician temple of Astarte and Temple 4 (floor 2a)

of use of the temple as such, though there are some indications that this continued also for floor 1.

There is very little evidence to indicate the plan of the room which was constructed above the floor 2 temple. Part of a floor 1 wall survives in the north-east corner and this at least indicates that the area was still in use as an enclosed room.

A new wall with foundation blocks of soft yellow stone, was constructed for floor 1. It lies to the east of and runs parallel to the eastern wall of the temple of earlier floors. There is an entrance to the south where the plaster of floor 1 is preserved. It is not clear whether this wall was built as the eastern border of the floor 1 room or whether it is a wall outside the room.

There are two other structures which belong to floor 1. One is a very large rectangular construction of local marmara, the original significance of which remains obscure. It stands against the north wall in the eastern end of the room. It actually lies upon the wall for floor 3 and the surviving stones of the walls of floor 1 and later periods are built at right-angles to it. As it stands now it measures 1·40 m (east–west) by 1·70 m (north–south) and 1·15 m in height and is constructed of three courses of local marmara blocks. This structure belongs to an early phase of floor 1, as is evident from its relation to the second structure belonging to the floor: this is a concrete channel which runs against the east and north sides of the marmara structure and the wall and then turns at right-angles to cross above the Late Bronze Age city wall. It is 50 cm wide and contained Hellenistic sherds. As its direction and shape are dictated by the presence of the table it must have been built when the table was already in existence. The marmara structure by itself looks like a table of offerings or even an altar. However no traces of burning or other altar debris were found.

Above floor 1 are the Hellenistic and Roman floors. The only evidence for the constructions of these later periods, the last in the use of the area, is again the small section of wall preserved to the north-east which appears to have been rebuilt.

In the area to the south of Temple 4 a bothros (bothros 17) has been excavated. It measures 8 m × 5 m and is 45 cm deep and it contained material corresponding to floor 2a of Temple 4. It produced many sherds and whole vases (juglets, bowls, miniature juglets and cups) of Plain White ware and terracotta figurines, some of

Plate 104

the 'Astarte' type, as well as patches of charcoal, animal bones including a sheeps' horn and impressions of *pinolia* seeds. The most interesting contents of bothros 17 are a twelve-sided column (2·20 m long and 39–42 cm in diameter) and a capital of local gypsum. The style

Plate 105

of the capital, with its carved papyrus leaf decoration, is Egyptian in inspiration. Similar but smaller columns and capitals are known

Plate 106

from Palaepaphos. They also appear on a clay model of a sanctuary from Idalion, now in the Louvre, on either side of the doorway as free-standing columns.

Who was the deity worshipped in Temple 4? A terracotta figurine showing the well-known goddess with lifted arms, found in Temple 4 in a layer which is dateable to the eleventh century BC, is identical with those found in a bothros just outside the north wall of the great temple of Astarte. The 'Astarte'-type figurines of bothros 17 are again of the same type as those found in other bothroi belonging to the temple of Astarte. This evidence may suggest that Temple 4, at least during the Phoenician period (if not also during the earlier periods), was also dedicated to Astarte.

Temple 4 is unique, not only in its architectural plan, its altars and the material which it has produced, but also because of the fact that it offers a valuable stratification for dating. Its continuous use from the end of the thirteenth century to *c.* 1000 BC and then from the middle of the ninth century BC to 312 BC and even later, provides a unique opportunity for the study of evolution in architectural ideas as well as for the chronological appreciation of the material which its superimposed floors have produced. In this respect it may be compared with the temple of Keos which was constantly in use from the fifteenth cetury BC to the Hellenistic period.[102]

Excavations at Kition will no doubt continue in the future and a new sacred area may be brought to light, centring round Temple 4, as the paved area east of the holy-of-holies would suggest. But with the architectural remains uncovered already and with the wealth of material at our disposal we believe that we may offer an adequate picture of the archaeology of Kition from the earliest period down to the end of the Phoenician period. Future excavations will doubtless enrich our knowledge of the history of the town and its material culture, but it is unlikely that any radical changes will occur.

VI Built Tombs of Kition

Apart from the architectural remains described in earlier chapters, no other remains of Kition are now visible; those discovered by the Swedish Cyprus Expedition about forty-five years ago have disappeared completely. There are, however, several built tombs worthy of mention,[103] one of them discovered during recent years. They had all been looted and do not provide further evidence of burial customs.

One of the best-known tombs of Kition is situated on the southern extremity of the ancient town, where a chapel known as the chapel of Ayia Phaneromeni was constructed in 1907. Several travellers and scholars of the eighteenth and nineteenth centuries were intrigued by the monumentality of this building and attempted to interpret it in various ways. M. Ohnefalsch-Richter suggested that this structure, erected over a previously existing spring, may have been a kind of Nymphaeum. He gave a similar interpretation for a comparable structure in the necropolis of Salamis (Tomb 50, known as the 'Tomb' or 'Prison of St Catherine').[104] The built tombs of Salamis and those of Tamassos now help us to a better understanding of the architecture of this tomb. It consists of two rectangular chambers, probably with a dromos in front. The dromos, however, and the outer chamber have been partly demolished owing to the construction of the chapel and the use of the tomb itself as a place of worship with an icon of Panayia Phaneromeni in the inner chamber.

The tomb was constructed out of enormous blocks of hard limestone, within a large and deep ditch cut in the rock, in the fashion of all the built tombs of Salamis of the eighth and seventh centuries BC. Both chambers are rectangular, the inner one having a rounded corner. There are no traces of the façade or the door of the outer chamber. The two chambers are separated by a thick wall provided

Fig. 20

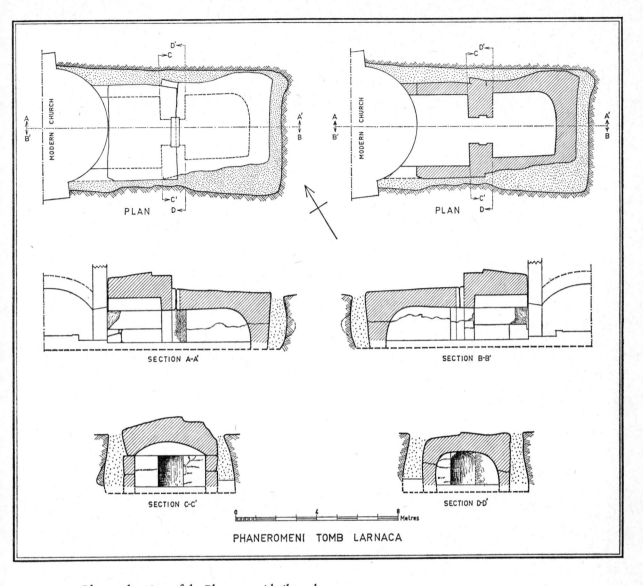

PLAN

MODERN CHURCH

PLAN

MODERN CHURCH

SECTION A-A'

SECTION B-B'

SECTION C-C'

SECTION D-D'

0   4   8 Metres

PHANEROMENI TOMB LARNACA

20 *Plans and sections of the Phaneromeni built tomb*

with a sliding portcullis-door, lowered by a special mechanism through an opening in the roof, in the same way as the portcullis-door of the 'Tomb of Saint Catherine' at Salamis, where this arrangement is dated to the early Christian period. But, as in the case of the Salamis tomb, the portcullis-door in the Phaneromeni tomb may be a later addition to an earlier tomb, probably dated to the seventh or sixth centuries BC. It is interesting to note that as in the case of the

Salamis tomb, this structure never lost its sanctity, and is still used today as a place of worship.

The megalithic construction of the Phaneromeni tomb is less imposing than that of the Salamis tomb, but it is not of less interest. Two enormous blocks cover the roof of both chambers. The one covering the roof of the inner chamber measures 4·65 m × 4·50 m; its maximum thickness is 2·70 m and its minimum thickness 90 cm. The second stone covering the outer chamber measures 3·35 m × 4·60 m; maximum thickness 1·65 m, minimum 95 cm. They are hollowed at the lower part to form a vaulted roof. The inner chamber measures 3·26 m in length, 3·10 m in width and 1·95 m in height. The width of the outer chamber is 3·40 m and its height 2·50 m; its length is preserved to 2·50 m.

There is no evidence at Kition for a 'Royal Cemetery' with built tombs as there is at Salamis. But the Phaneromeni tomb and the continuation in later periods of the tradition of built tombs in this town does not exclude such a hypothesis.

Fig. 21

In 1972 a large built tomb was accidentally discovered during building operations at a site known as 'Tourabi', the large Archaic and Classical cemetery in the western part of Kition. This tomb (no·9) had been looted already but its architecture made it worthwhile excavating. The tomb may have been built originally in the late Classical or Hellenistic period, and was used continuously throughout the Hellenistic and Roman periods. Attic Black-Glazed pottery and Ptolemaic coins found in the chamber may attest its early date, but the later usage was Roman (second–third centuries AD). It is a

Figs 22–25

large chamber, built of local gypsum slabs, measuring 4·50 m in length, 3·50 m in width and 2·50 m in height. Its original entrance was to the west, but this was later (during the Roman period?) blocked up and a new entrance with a stepped dromos was constructed on the south side. This new entrance was shaped like a doorway, with two large gypsum slabs forming the door. At the northern side there is a vaulted recess, obviously for the sarcophagus of the original burial.

The roof of the chamber is flat, made of large well-dressed gypsum slabs, drafted along the edges to resemble planks of wood. The floor

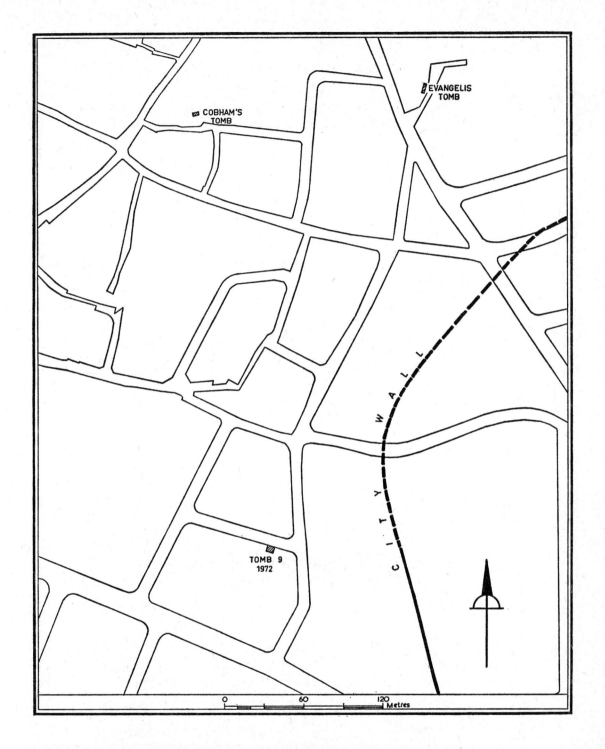

21 *Site plan showing the three built tombs in the 'Tourabi' cemetery to the west of*
Kition

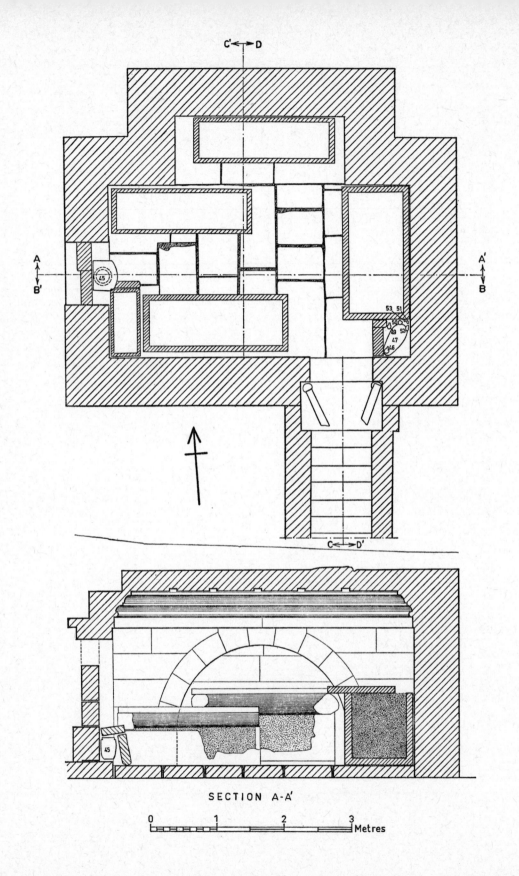

C' ←→ D

A ←↕→ B'

A' ←↕→ B

45

53 51
50
49 52
47
46

C ←→ D'

SECTION A-A'

0   1   2   3
Metres

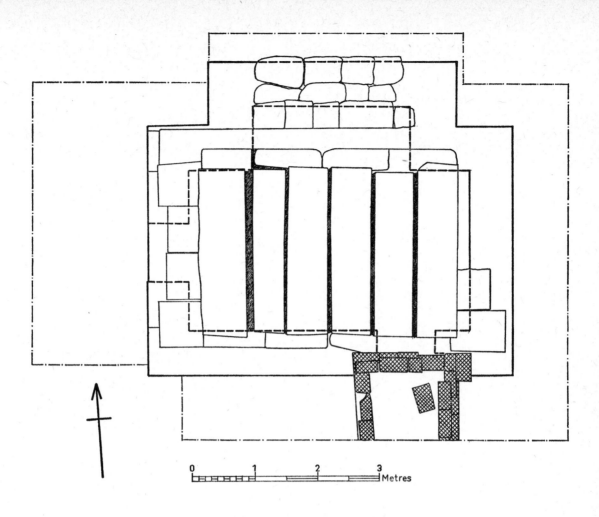

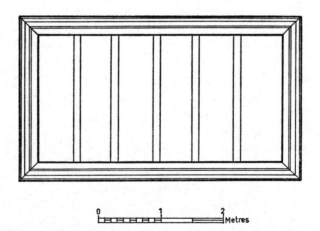

22 Opposite, *plan and section of built Tomb 9 (excavated in 1972) in the 'Tourabi'*
cemetery

23, 24 Above, *plan of the roof of Tomb 9.* Below, *plan of the ceiling of Tomb 9*

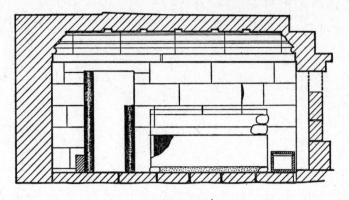

SECTION B-B'

0 1 2 3
Metres

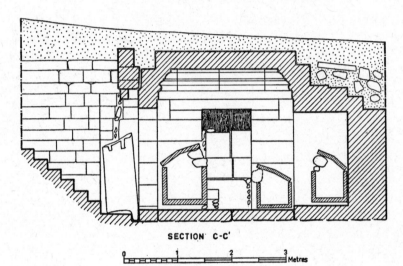

SECTION C-C'

0 1 2 3
Metres

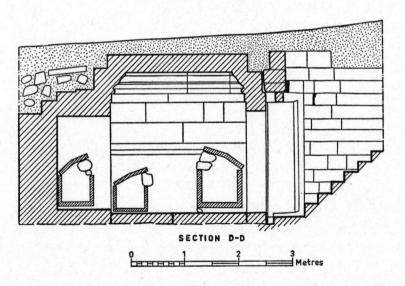

SECTION D-D

0 1 2 3
Metres

25 *Sections of the chamber of Tomb 9*

was of limestone slabs. The walls are constructed of regular dry-set blocks of gypsum. Along the top of the walls, on all four sides, there is a well-carved frieze with mouldings of fine quality.

Five sarcophagi were found in the tomb, carved out of hard gypsum blocks. The burials inside them had previously been looted for gold, but large quantities of glass vessels, pottery, clay lamps, coins and some bronze objects (mainly mirrors) were found in the fill of the chamber. One small limestone sarcophagus was found intact. It contained the skeleton of a very young girl, with her gold ear-rings and gold finger-ring *in situ*. There were also small glass bottles. She held a bronze coin (an *obolos*) in her hand. Against the western wall of the chamber, well hidden with slabs, was a cylindrical lead box with its lid on, containing incinerated skeletal remains and two glass bottles.

Two other built tombs have long been known within the area of ancient Kition and have often been described by scholars.[105] They had been looted and there is no external evidence for their dating apart from their architecture. One of them is known as the 'Evangelis tomb' and lies outside the west walls of Kition, in the 'Tourabi' cemetery. It has two rectangular chambers, one behind the other; part of the outer chamber as well as the dromos were damaged. The chambers were built of well-dressed stones and had corbelled vaults built of large blocks in a fashion which recalls the Cypro–Archaic Tomb 19 of the Salamis cemetery and a tomb at Xylotymbou, not far from Kition.[106] This comparison may suggest a Cypro–Archaic or Cypro–Classical date for the tomb, though it may have also been used in later times. Three sarcophagi were found in the innermost chamber.

Fig. 26

The two chambers communicate with one another through a narrow doorway. The innermost chamber measures 2·32 m in length, 2·35 m in width and 2·15 m in height. The outer chamber is 2·35 m wide and its length is preserved to 4·60 m.

The last tomb to be described is known as 'Cobham's tomb' and lies at a short distance from the Evangelis tomb. Its architectural plan is almost complete: a stepped dromos leads to three chambers, one behind the other and on the same axis. They are all rectangular

Fig. 27

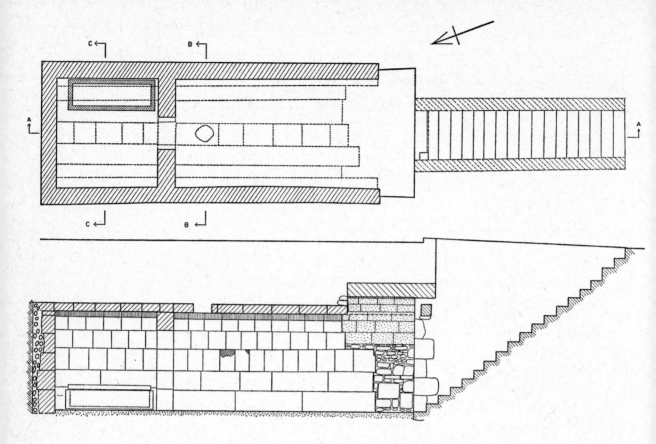

SECTION A-A

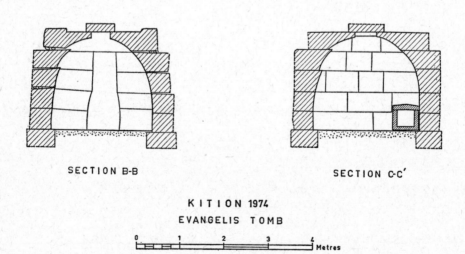

SECTION B-B

SECTION C-C'

KITION 1974
EVANGELIS TOMB

0   1   2   3   4
Metres

26 *Plan and sections of 'Evangelis' tomb (after Jeffrey)*

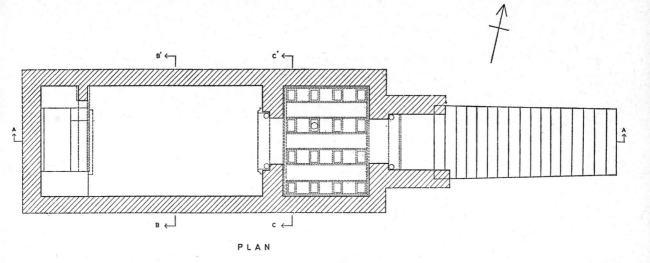

PLAN

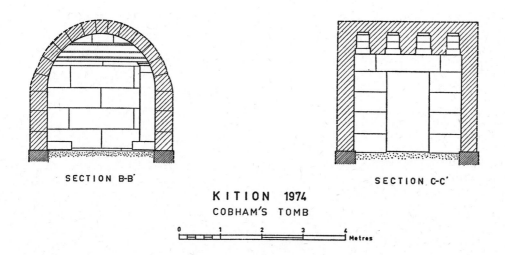

SECTION A-A'

SECTION B-B'

SECTION C-C'

KITION 1974
COBHAM'S TOMB

0   1   2   3   4
Metres

27   Plan and sections of 'Cobham's' tomb (after Jeffrey)

and measure 2·03 m × 2·60 m (outermost chamber), 4·23 m × 2·60 m, 89 cm × 2·60 m (innermost chamber). The dromos is 1·30 m wide and is preserved to a length of 1·38 m. The tomb is constructed very neatly with regular courses of ashlar blocks. The first (outer) chamber had a very fine coffered ceiling, whereas the other two chambers are provided with semi-circular barrel vaults. On both sides of the doorways between the chambers there are mouldings against the walls in the form of pilaster capitals. These features suggests a rather late date for this tomb, probably Roman.

No doubt more built tombs may be found in the 'Tourabi' cemetery in the western part of the modern town of Larnaca, where three are already known. This is a densely populated part of the town and only when old houses are pulled down for the construction of new ones is archaeological investigation possible.

75 Two pits for sacred trees arranged symmetrically on either side of the entrance to the temenos of the great Phoenician temple, floor 3

76 Base of a Samaria ware bowl found on floor 3 of the great Phoenician temple

77 A general view of bothros 9 in the temenos of the great Phoenician temple, showing piles of broken pottery

78 A Samaria ware double bowl of extraordinarily large dimensions, found in bothros 12 of the courtyard of the great Phoenician temple

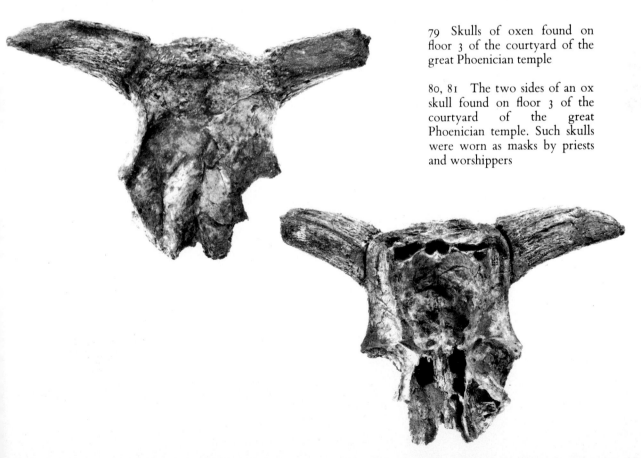

79 Skulls of oxen found on floor 3 of the courtyard of the great Phoenician temple

80, 81 The two sides of an ox skull found on floor 3 of the courtyard of the great Phoenician temple. Such skulls were worn as masks by priests and worshippers

82 Clay figures from the precinct of the temple of Apollo at Kourion showing priests or worshippers wearing bulls' masks

83 A fragmentary Red Slip ware bowl with an engraved Phoenician inscription on its outer surface. It was found on floor 3 of the courtyard of the great Phoenician temple

84　A deposit of miniature vases *in situ* in the south-west corner of the courtyard of the temple of Astarte, floor 3

85　A pillar base in the courtyard of the temple of Astarte, floor 2a (above, right); next to it (below, left) is a base of the previous period, floor 3

86 An altar in the temenos of the temple of Astarte, floor 2a

87 The ivory hilt of a sword with silver-plated rivets. Found on floor 2a of the courtyard of the temple of Astarte

88 Statuette of a kneeling woman, made of faience. It was used as a flask to hold water of the Nile ('eau de juvence')

89 Bronze statuette found outside the courtyard of the temple of Astarte in a layer corresponding to floor 2a

90 Faience figurine representing the Egyptian god Bes. From a bothros corresponding to the third period of the temple of Astarte

91 Gypsum altar in front of the south entrance to the courtyard of the temple of Astarte, floor 2. The entrance (left) was blocked during the subsequent period

92 Fragment of a sixth-century bowl with an engraved Phoenician inscription mentioning the name of Melkarth (Heracles). Found in a bothros outside the temple of Astarte

93   Three hearths in the temenos of the temple of Astarte, floor 2

94, 95   Gold coin of Pumiathon, king of Kition (enlarged). On the obverse (94), Heracles-Melkarth holds a club and bowl, with an *ankh* below. On the reverse (95), a lion is attacking a stag

96, 97 Attic pottery fragments of large craters found in bothroi of the Phoenician temple of Astarte, associated with the third period

98, 99 Terracotta statuettes found in bothroi of the last Phoenician temple of Astarte, corresponding to the third period (see also Plate 101)

100 Limestone statuette (top, right) betraying the influence of Greek sculpture, from a bothros of the last Phoenician temple of Astarte

101 Bothros containing terracottas and limestone statuettes, corresponding to the last period of the temple of Astarte

◀ 102 Altar C of Temple 4, floor 3

◀ 103 View of Temple 4, floor 2a,
from the east with altars A and B near
the centre of the courtyard. Next to one
of the altars is a table of offerings
(foreground, left) belonging to floor 1

104 Terracotta figurine of the Astarte
type found in bothros 17 of Temple 4

105 Fragmentary capital in an
Egyptianizing style from bothros 17 of
Temple 4

106 Clay model of a sanctuary from Idalion, Cyprus, now in the Louvre, showing two free-standing columns on either side of the entrance. The capitals are of an Egyptianizing style

VII Religious Aspects of Kition

The sacred buildings at Kition occupy an important part of the excavated remains in Area II at the northern part of the site. Four temples have so far been uncovered, with two sacred courtyards which were in use during the Late Bronze Age. Two of the temples were also used as such throughout the Phoenician period. The sacred character of the site, therefore, has a history of more than 700 years, during which a great variety of religious concepts and ideas were developed which illustrate the diversity of the cultural character of Cyprus. The small Temples 2 and 3 appear at the very beginning of the history of the site, early in the thirteenth century BC. Built near the city wall, with a sacred garden between them, they may have already been associated with a metallurgical cult, though no definitive proof for this has yet come to light. Copper must have been smelted in the area, however, judging from the quantities of copper slag discovered in association with early thirteenth-century material under floor III of Temenos A. This may be supported by the location of the temples near the city wall, where metallurgical workshops were usually built. No material has been found from this early period in the life of the city which could be directly associated with any cult in these two temples other than a large number of votive stone anchors, which were used as building material in constructions of the subsequent period (floor III). Ships transported the copper from the harbour of Kition to the outside world and any god of metallurgy should naturally be associated with the navigators who played such an important role in the copper trade.

We have more concrete evidence about the character of the cult in the temples of Kition during the subsequent period, from the end of the thirteenth century BC down to the very end of the Late Bronze Age and the beginning of the Iron Age. The discovery of

Plate XIV

workshops for the smelting of copper in the proximity of Temples 1 and 2 and Temene A and B and the direct communication between the industrial and the sacred area illustrate most clearly the association of religion with metallurgy, known from a number of other sites both in Cyprus and the Near East. In prehistoric times, namely in the Early Bronze Age, the gods protected agriculture and were symbolized by the bull which is associated with the fertility of the soil. In the Late Bronze Age, which may be characterized as the period of industrial development, religion follows new trends and the gods protect the copper mines of the island; they become smith-gods. The old fertility goddess now stands on a base in the form of an oxhide ingot of copper, symbolizing the fertility of the mines. Religion is conditioned by the new aspects of economic development which is based on copper trade. The gods protected metallurgy but probably at the same time the state, based on a religious structure, could easily control the export of copper which was the backbone of the island's economy. This association of religion with copper may also be symbolized by the foundation deposit of two bronze agricultural tools and a bronze peg discovered in the north-west corner of Temple 4.

The Near Eastern character of the Late Bronze Age culture of Cyprus is great in spite of the undisputed fact that during this period the island underwent a profound cultural change as a result of the Achaean colonization. Deeply rooted Near Eastern concepts in religious matters persist, even during a period when Aegean influences are strong and widespread. The plan of the temples is essentially Near Eastern and the idea of the sacred gardens may also be rooted in the East. There are, however, certain religious features which illustrate the influx of Aegean ideas. The horns of consecration, of which two examples have been found in the two temene of the sacred area, are a case in point. These may have been associated with tables of offerings or altars for bloodless sacrifices, whereas sacrifices of animals were carried out on separate altars.

The identification of the gods or goddesses who were worshipped in the temples of Kition during the Late Bronze Age cannot be determined as no iconographical vestiges have been discovered.

Plate 56

Plates 59, XV

Plates 48, 51

Their identity, however, may be inferred from the existence of two
bronze statuettes from Cyprus, one from Enkomi and both dating to
the twelfth century B C. These represent a male and a female deity,
each standing on a base in the form of an oxhide ingot.

Plates 55, 56

Towards the very end of the Late Bronze Age and the beginning
of the Iron Age the prevailing deity worshipped in one or more of
three temples of the site (Temples 1, 2 and 4) must have been a
female deity under strong Aegean, mainly Cretan, influence. She is
a fertility goddess, with prominent breasts and lifted arms, obviously
the Cretan goddess who may have been imported to the island after
the 'Dorian invasion' from Crete and was identified with the old
Cypriote fertility goddess.

Plate 65

Kition is a unique example where the continuity in the sanctity
of a sacred site can be observed. After 150 years of abandonment of
the sacred area, the Phoenicians built their temple of the goddess
Astarte on the foundations of the old Temple 1, which was probably
also a temple of the fertility goddess. From the middle of the ninth
century to the end of the fourth century B C, this temple area was
the centre of religious life in the town and was one of the most
important in the whole island. The religious life of the town is now
centred round the cult of Astarte, the goddess established as the
divinity *par excellence* of the Phoenician world by Ethbaal, king of
the Sidonians. She was to dominate the religion of Cyprus for more
than 500 years.

Architecturally the temple of Astarte is the largest Phoenician
temple discovered so far in the Phoenician world and it illustrates the
fine workmanship of Tyrian masonry, giving an idea of how the
temple of Solomon in Jerusalem, also built by Tyrian masons,
would have looked. The numerous skulls of oxen, worn as masks
during ceremonies, which have been found on the earliest floor of
the temple, illustrate part of the ritual which was performed by the
priests of the goddess under the spacious porticos of its courtyard.
This custom evokes a very old tradition in Cypriote religion and
revives the cult of the bull as symbolizing fertility, a cult which has
its roots in the Early Cypriote Bronze Age. The inscribed bowl
which mentions Astarte and the sacrifice in her honour by a citizen

Plates 79-81

of Tamassos is a vivid testimony which may evoke customs known from other places of the ancient world, where the cutting and dedication of hair in honour of the gods was also practised. The temple of Astarte must have been frequented by large numbers of worshippers from not only Cyprus and from the Near East, but also from the Aegean. The numerous offerings found in the *bothroi* which correspond to the various phases of the temple are characteristic of its wealth. Fine Phoenician dishes of Samaria ware, Greek oil-jars from Attica, Egyptian scarabs and amulets, illustrate the cosmopolitan character of Kition throughout the Phoenician period.

Plates 76, 78, 96, 97
Plate XX

Two temples exist side by side during the whole of the Phoenician period; the great temple of Astarte and Temple 4. So far no indications have come to light regarding the identification of the deity worshipped in the second, smaller Temple 4. The old association between religion and metallurgy was not, however, completely forgotten. The discovery of a workshop for the smelting of copper, corresponding to the Archaic and Classical periods and situated next to the old east entrance to the great temple of Astarte, may be considered as a survival of this Late Bronze Age concept. Smiths must have had their workshops next to the temple to produce bronze figurines which were sold to the worshippers.

The fall of the Phoenician dynasty of Kition at the end of the fourth century BC coincides with the end of the use of the sacred area. It is quite characteristic that Ptolemy I, who killed the last Phoenician king of Kition, Pumiathon, set fire to the Phoenician temples which illustrated above all else the domination of the Phoenicians over the city.

Table I: Chronological list of periods and events in Areas I and II (above right)

Table II: Floor levels at Kition and related finds and events (below right)

AREA I

		PERIOD	AEGEAN	REMARKS
A *Tombs*		1. Early Bronze Age III 2000–1850 BC (Tombs 6–8)	Early Helladic III	*Red Polished and Black Polished pottery. Scarcity of bronzes*
		2. Late Cypriote IIB 1300–1230 BC (Tombs 4 and 5, 9)	Late Helladic IIIB	*Trade with the Near East and the Aegean. Abundance of Mycenaean pottery, luxury goods from the East*
B *Buildings*	FLOORS IV	Late Cypriote IIB 1300–1230 BC	Late Helladic IIIB	*Trade with the East and the Aegean*
	III	Late Cypriote IIIA 1230–1190 BC	Late Helladic IIIC	*First Achaean colonists*
	II	Late Cypriote IIIB–C 1190–1050 BC	Late Helladic IIIC– Sub-Mycenaean	*Sea Peoples' invasions; second wave of Achaean colonists; destruction by earthquake*
	I	Cypro–Geometric 1050–1000 BC	Protogeometric	*Reconstruction of buildings*

AREA II

A *Tombs*		Early Bronze Age III 2000–1850 BC (Tombs 1–8)	Early Helladic III	*Red Polished and Black Polished pottery. Scarcity of bronzes*

FLOORS		PERIOD	IDENTIFICATION	AEGEAN AND THE EAST	REMARKS
	IV	Late Cypriote IIB 1300–1230 BC	Temples 2 and 3, mudbrick city wall, bastions	Late Helladic IIIB	*Sacred gardens. Mycenaean IIIB pottery*
	III	Late Cypriote IIIA 1230–1190 BC	Temples 1, 2 and 4. Cyclopean city wall, workshops	Late Helladic IIIC	*Ashlar block constructions, sacred gardens. Mycenaean IIIC: 1 pottery*
	II	Late Cypriote IIIB–C 1190–1050 BC	Temples 1, 2 and 4. City wall, workshops	Late Helladic IIIC– Sub-Mycenaean	*Proto-White Painted pottery*
B *Buildings*	I	Cypro-Geometric I 1050–1000 BC	Temples 1, 2 and 4	Protogeometric	*Cypro–Geometric I pottery. Cemetery in Sotiros quarter*
	3	Cypro-Geometric III c. 850–800 BC	Phoenician Temples 1 and 4	Late Geometric. Phoenician expansion to the West	*Samaria ware pottery. Phoenician inscription from the temple of Astarte*
	2a	Cypro–Geometric III– Cypro–Archaic I 800–600 BC	Phoenician Temples 1 and 4	Orientalizing period in Greece. Conquest of Cyprus by Sargon II (709 BC)	*Bothroi. Imports from Greece and from Phoenicia*
	2	Cypro–Archaic I– Cypro–Classical I 600–450 BC	Phoenician Temples 1 and 4	Wars against the Persians. The Phoenician conquest of Idalion	*Bothroi. Imports from Attica and from Phoenicia*
	I	Cypro–Classical I– Hellenistic I 450–312 BC	Phoenician Temples 1 and 4	Tamassos sold to Kition. Ptolemies. Destruction of Phoenician temples	*Imports from Attica and from Phoenicia*

Notes

Foreword

1 For a short, comprehensive account on the Late Bronze Age in Cyprus and relevant bibliography see H. W. Catling, 'Cyprus in the Neolithic and the Bronze Age periods', *Cambridge Ancient History* (revised edit. of Vols. I and II, 1966), 49 ff.

2 For a report on the discoveries of 1959 see V. Karageorghis, in *Bulletin de Correspondance Hellénique* 84 (1960), 504–88.

3 Regular preliminary reports on the excavations at Kition appear yearly in the *Bulletin de Correspondance Hellénique*.

4 Cf. *Bulletin de Correspondance Hellénique* 84 (1960), 407.

5 For biblical references to Kition see Sir George Hill, *A History of Cyprus* (1940), 96 ff.; E. Gjerstad, *The Swedish Cyprus Expedition* IV: 2 (1948), 436, 459; H. Jacob Katzenstein, *The History of Tyre* (1973), *sub verbum*.

6 An exception will be made when we discuss the built tombs of Kition, which may now be interpreted in a new light, mainly as a result of the excavation of the built tombs of the Royal Necropolis of Salamis.

Chapter I

7 For a preliminary report on the first season of excavations see *Bulletin de Correspondance Hellénique* 97 (1973), 695 f.; the first volume on the results of earlier excavations and new research on Kition is now in preparation and will be published in the series *Studies in Mediterranean Archaeology*, edited by Professor Paul Åström.

8 See P. Dikaios, *Enkomi* II (1971), 895 ff.

9 For references see V. Karageorghis, 'Chypre', in *L'espansione Fenicia nel Mediterraneo* (1971), 161 ff.

10 E. Gjerstad *et al.*, *The Swedish Cyprus Expedition* III, 1.

11 *Ibid.* 74.

12 See *Bulletin de Correspondance Hellénique* 84 (1960), 507 for references.

13 *Ibid.*

14 For an account of this operation see D. M. Bailey in *The British Museum Quarterly* XXXIV (1969), 36 ff.

15 We shall refer to this inscription in Chapter V below.

16 Cf. Sir George Hill, *op. cit.*, 104 ff.

17 For a list of excavations at Kition and short reports see J. L. Myres and M. Ohnefalsch-Richter, *A Catalogue of the Cyprus Museum* (1899),

5 f.; J. L. Myres, in *The Annual of the British School at Athens* 41 (1940–45), 85 ff.

18 Olivier Masson and Maurice Sznycer, *Recherches sur les Phéniciens à Chypre* (1972), 21 ff.

19 Alexander Drummond, *Travels* (1754), 153.

20 Richard Pococke, *A description of the East, etc.* (1755), 213.

21 Plans of the walls of Kition as well as an indication of the harbour are given both by Pococke (*ibid.*, pl. XXXII) and by Giovanni Mariti, *Viaggi per l'isola di Cipro* (1769), frontispiece.

22 *Bulletin de Correspondance Hellénique* 84 (1960), 508 f.

23 The material from the newly excavated Early Bronze Age tombs of Kition is published by the present writer in *Excavations at Kition* I. *The Tombs* (1974).

Chapter II

24 Cf. C. F. A. Schaeffer, *Missions en Chypre, 1932–1935* (1936), 83 ff.

Chapter III

25 Cf. G. Mylonas, in *American Journal of Archaeology* 52 (1948), 70; *idem, Archaeologikon Deltion* 19 (1964), 89.

26 For a survey of this controversial subject see V. Karageorghis, F. Asaro, I. Perlman, in *Archäologischer Anzeiger* (1972), 188 ff., with relevant bibliography.

27 Cf. J. Tzedakis in *Acts of the First International Congress of Cypriote Studies* (1972), 163 ff. For a general survey of the problem cf. also H. W. Catling and V. Karageorghis in *The Annual of the British School at Athens* 55 (1960), 125 ff.

28 For a detailed discussion on shapes of Mycenaean vases which appear only in the Levantine region see V. Karageorghis, *Nouveaux Documents pour l'Etude de Bronze Récent à Chypre* (1965), 201 ff.

29 Published by V. Karageorghis in *Archäologischer Anzeiger* (1967), 162 ff.

30 See *idem, The Annual of the British School at Athens* 52 (1957), 38 ff. The fourth vase by this painter is illustrated in Dikaios, *Enkomi*, pl. 299:5.

31 *The Journal of Egyptian Archaeology* 58 (1972), 284, pl. XLV; 59 (1973), 233.

32 A complete study of these skulls by Jeffrey H. Schwartz appears in Appendix I in V. Karageorghis, *Excavations at Kition* I. *The Tombs* (1974).

33 Cf. H.-G. Buchholz, in *Bronze Age Migrations in the Aegean* (1974), 179 ff; P. Åström, *The Swedish Cyprus Expedition* IV:1D, 772.

34 Cf. J. L. Benson, *Bamboula at Kourion* (1972), 108, n. 8.

35 This painter has been presented by V. Karageorghis in *Alasia* I (1971), 123 ff.

36 Discussed in detail by V. Karageorghis in *Nouveaux Documents pour*

l'*Etude du Bronze Récent à Chypre*, 157 ff.; see also Dikaios, *Enkomi* II, 841 ff.

37 Cf. H. L. Lorimer, *Homer and the Monuments*, 111 f.; Sp. Iakovides, *Perati* II, 377 f.; R. Maxwell-Hyslop, in *Iraq* 36 (1974), 139 ff. It is possible that Anatolia may be the source of iron for the Near East in the Late Bronze Age.

38 For the problem of the relations between Cyprus and Egypt during the Late Bronze Age see Y. Lynn Holmes in *Orient and Occident* (Essays presented to Cyrus H. Gordon on the occasion of his sixty-fifth birthday, edit. Harry A. Hoffner, Jr, 1973), 91 ff.; R. S. Merrillees, *The Cypriote pottery found in Egypt* (1968). 186, 202.

39 We owe this identification to Dr Eitan Tchernov of the Department of Zoology, the Hebrew University of Jerusalem.

40 For further examples and convenient references see G. R. H. Wright, in *Palestine Exploration Quarterly* (1971), 17 ff.

41 E.g. at a recently excavated sacred area at Kamid el-Loz in the Lebanon (R. Hachmann and A. Kuschke, *Kamid el-Loz 1963/64* (1966), 57, figs 21:4 and 23:12).

42 Cf. *ibid.*, fig. 20:9; G. Loud, *The Megiddo ivories* (1939), pl. 12, 45–53.

43 Published by V. Karageorghis and Emilia Masson in *Biblioteca di antichità cipriote* I (1971), 237 ff.

44 For references to such temples see V. Karageorghis, 'Kition, Mycenaean and Phoenician', *Proceedings of the British Academy* 59 (1973), 9n. 3.

45 See J. Vandier *Manuel d'Archéologie Egyptienne* II, 689, 720 f. For a general discussion on sacred gardens see W. Andrae, in *Die Welt des Orients* I (1952), 6 ff.

46 *Strabo* XIV. 683 and 684.

47 E. Sjöqvist, in *Archiv für Religionswissenschaft* 30 (1932), 348 ff.

Chapter IV

48 Cf. R. Carpenter, *Discontinuity in Greek civilization* (1966); C. F. A. Schaeffer, *Ugaritica* V (1968), 760 ff.

49 For city walls of this period see P. Åström, *The Swedish Cyprus Expedition* IV: 1C, 40 ff.

50 Such votive anchors were also found in the precinct of the Late Bronze Age temple of Baal at Ras Shamra.

51 Vandier, *op. cit.*

52 J. du Plat Taylor *et al.*, *Myrtou-Pigadhes* (1957), 103 ff.

53 Cf. Carl W. Blegen and Marion Rawson, *The Palace of Nestor at Pylos in Western Messenia* I, 301 ff.

54 See V. Karageorghis in *Athens Annals of Archaeology* 4 (1971), 101 ff.

55 See C. F. A. Schaeffer, in *Archiv für Orientforschung* 21 (1966), 59 ff.; *idem*, in *Antiquity* 39 (1965), 56 f.

56 H. W. Catling, in *Alasia* I, 15 ff.

57 Trude Dothan and A. Ben-Tor, in *Israel Exploration Journal* 22 (1972), 201 ff.

58 Published by Beno Rothenberg, *Timna, Valley of the Biblical Copper Mines* (1972).

59 See Maurice Sznycer, in *Supplément au Dictionnaire de la Bible* VIII, fasc. 47 (1972), col. 1384 ff.

60 For references see V. Karageorghis, in *Acts of the International Archaeological Symposium 'The Mycenaeans in the Eastern Mediterranean'* (1973), 108 n. 10.

61 M. A. Hanfmann and Jane Waldbaum, in *Bulletin of American Schools of Oriental Research* 199 (1970), 7 ff., fig. 8.

62 Cf. G. R. H. Wright, in *Palestine Exploration Quarterly* (1971), 19 ff.

63 Cf. Dikaios, *Enkomi*, pls 35–36.

64 Richard Ellis, *Foundation Deposits in Ancient Mesopotamia* (1968).

65 Cf. Dikaios, *op. cit.*, 295 f.

66 Such tools are known elsewhere from Cyprus (H. W. Catling, *Cypriot Bronzework in the Mycenaean World* (1964), 80 ff., pl. 4: b, g. Cf. also *ibid.*, 272, pl. 50: a, a bronze mould for a plough-share.

67 Cf. Ellis, *op. cit.*, 46 ff.

68 Cf. Catling, *op. cit.*, pl. 52:b (25).

69 Cf. Ellis, *op. cit.*, fig. 32:b, d.

70 Cf. Dikaios, *Enkomi* II, 522 f.

71 Cf. *Ibid.*, 525 f., 532 f.

72 There is not general agreement about the cause of the abandonment of Enkomi. Dikaios believes that it was owing to the threat of hostile attacks against the town (*ibid.*, 534); Schaeffer (*Enkomi–Alasia* I, 315 ff.) believes that the cause was an earthquake and that soon after a hostile army chased away the last inhabitants of the town.

Chapter V

73 Cf. E. Gjerstad, *The Swedish Cyprus Expedition* IV :2, 436 ff., also for references about the possibility of an earlier date for the Phoenician colonization.

74 Cf. Marguerite Yon, *Salamine de Chypre II. La Tombe T.I du XIᵉ S. Av.J.-C.* (1971), 96.

75 Cf. S. Moscati, *The World of the Phoenicians* (1968), 103.

76 *Ibid.*, Katzenstein, *op. cit.*, 84 ff.

77 Gjerstad, *op. cit.*, 436 f.

78 See, however, a different view supported by Katzenstein, who believes that Khardihadast (New City) is Limassol, though he accepts that Kition was the first Tyrian colony in Cyprus (*op. cit.*, 85).

79 See A. Westholm, in *Acta Archaeologica* 4 (1933), 201 ff.

80 For references and similar features in an Israelite temple at Arad see Y. Aharoni, in *Biblical Archaeologist* 31 (1968), 18 ff.

81 These pillars are quite distinct on an Assyrian relief showing the escape of Luli, king of Sidon, from the city of Tyre. See R. D. Barnett, in *Eretz-Israel* 9 (1969), 7, pl. I:1 (extreme right).

82 As mentioned in the Bible (*Kings* 5:15–18).

83 Cf. V. Karageorghis, in *Rivista di Studi Fenici* I (1973), 12 f.

84 Cf. *idem*, in *Harvard Theological Review* 64 (1971), 261 ff.

85 *Ibid.*

86 A. Dupont-Sommer, in *Mémoires de l'Académie des Inscriptions et Belles-Lettres* 44 (1970), 1–24.

87 The same inscription was republished by B. Peckham, in *Orientalia* 37 (1968), 304 ff., and also by Olivier Masson and Maurice Sznycer, *Recherches sur les Phéniciens à Chypre* (1972), 21 ff.

88 I owe this suggestion to Professor B. Mazar, of the Hebrew University of Jerusalem, with whom I discussed the problems of the Phoenician temple of Kition in general. For references to Ethbaal see Katzenstein, *op. cit.*, 129 ff.

89 See note 79 above.

90 Herodotus I. 199. See also V. Karageorghis, in *Rivista di Studi Fenici* I (1973), 12.

91 For historical information about this period see E. Gjerstad, *The Swedish Cyprus Expedition* IV:2, 436 ff.; also Moscati, *op. cit.*, 104 ff.; Katzenstein, *op. cit.*, 240 ff.

92 Cf., however, note 78 above.

93 See Sir George Hill, *op. cit.*, 103 f.

94 Cf. V. Karageorghis, *Excavations in the Necropolis of Salamis* II (1970), 234 f.

95 Cf. *idem.*, *Excavations in the Necropolis of Salamis* I (1967), 43.

96 For the history of this period see E. Gjerstad, *The Swedish Cyprus Expedition* IV:2, 484 f.

97 Cf. V. Karageorghis and M.-G. Guzzo Amadasi, in *Rivista di Studi Fenici* I (1973), 93 f.; see also Gjerstad, *The Swedish Cyprus Expedition* IV:2, 462.

98 See Gjerstad, *The Swedish Cyprus Expedition* IV:2, 479 ff., also for the historical events during this period.

99 See Masson and Sznycer, *op. cit.*, 69 ff.

100 Gjerstad, *The Swedish Cyprus Expedition* IV:2, 501.

101 See V. Karageorghis and M.-G. Guzzo Amadasi, in *Rivista di Studi Fenici* I (1973), 129 ff.

102 Cf. John L. Caskey, in *Hesperia* 33 (1964), 314 ff., and *Hesperia* 35 (1966), 363 ff.

Chapter VI

103 Three of these tombs are described by A. Westholm in *Opuscula Archaeologica* I (1939), 39 ff.; where the reader is referred to for further bibliography.

104 Cf. V. Karageorghis, *Excavations in the Necropolis of Salamis* I, 90 ff.

105 Cf. G. Jeffery, in *Archaeologia* 66 (1915), 169 ff.

106 Cf. V. Karageorghis, *Excavations in the Necropolis of Salamis* I, 70 f., 122 f.

Select Bibliography

DUPONT-SOMMER, A. 'Une inscription phénicienne archaïque récemment trouvée à Kition (Chypre)', *Mémoires de l'Académie des Inscriptions et Belles-Lettres* 4 (1970), 1–28.

GALLING, K. 'Der Weg der Phöniker nach Tarsis', *Zeitschrift des Deutschen–Palästina-Vereins* 88 (1972), 142–7.

KARAGEORGHIS, V. Yearly reports in 'Chronique des fouilles et découvertes archéologiques à Chypre', *Bulletin de Correspondance Hellénique* since 1959.

—— 'Fouilles de Kition', *Bulletin de Correspondance Hellénique* 84 (1960), 504 ff.

—— 'New light on the history of ancient Kition', *Mélanges K. Michalowski* (1966), 495ff.

—— 'Fouilles de Kition, 1969', *Comptes Rendus à l' Académie des Inscriptions et Belles-Lettres* 44 (1970), 1–28.

—— 'Chypre', *L'Espansione Fenicia nel Mediterraneo* (1971), 161 ff.

—— The Mycenaeans at Kition, a preliminary survey', *Biblioteca di antichità cipriote* I (1971), 217 ff.

——'Contribution to the religion of Cyprus in the thirteenth and twelfth centuries BC', *Acts of the International Archaeological Symposium 'The Mycenaeans in the Eastern Mediterranean'* (1973), 105 ff.

—— 'Kition, Mycenaean and Phoenician' (Mortimer Wheeler Archaeological Lecture, British Academy, 1973), *Proceedings of the British Academy* IX (1973).

—— 'Le quartier sacré de Kition: campagne de fouilles 1972 et 1973', *Comptes Rendus à l'Académie des Inscriptions et Belles-Lettres* (1973), 520–30.

—— *Excavations at Kition* I. *The Tombs* (1974), 1–178, pls I-CLXXIX.

KARAGEORGHIS, V. and E. MASSON. 'Un bronze votif inscrit (modèle de foie ou de rein?) trouvé à Kition en 1970', *Biblioteca di antichità cipriote* I (1971), 237 ff.

KARAGEORGHIS, V. and M. – G. GUZZO AMADASI. 'Un iscrizione Fenicia da Cipro', *Rivista di Studi Fenici* I (1973), 129–34.

KATZENSTEIN, H. J. *The History of Tyre* (1973), *passim*.

MASSON, O. and M. SZNYCER. *Recherches sur les Phéniciens à Chypre* (1972).

MOSCATI, S. *I Fenici e Cartagine* (1972), *passim*.

PECKHAM, B. 'Notes on a fifth-century Phoenician inscription from Kition, Cyprus (CIS 86)', *Orientalia* 37 (1968), 304 ff.

List of Illustrations

Unless otherwise acknowledged illustrations are by courtesy of the Department of Antiquities, Cyprus.

Colour Plates

Monochrome Plates

Figures

The plans and sections are the work of Mr Elias Markou and Mr Chrysilios Polykarpou, Surveyors of the Department of Antiquities, Cyprus.

Index